UNAPOLOGETIC
Wealth

REWRITE YOUR MONEY STORY FROM ANY BEGINNING

MARCIA DAWOOD

Award-winning Author of
Do Good While Doing Well

Copyright © 2026 Marcia Dawood

All rights reserved. No part of this publication in print or in electronic format may be reproduced, stored in a retrieval system, or transmitted in any form or by any means, electronic, mechanical, photocopying, recording, or otherwise without the prior written permission of the publisher.

NO AI/NO BOT. The author does not consent to any Artificial Intelligence (AI), generative AI, large language model, machine learning, chatbot, or other automated analysis, generative process, or replication program to reproduce, mimic, remix, summarize, or otherwise replicate any part of this creative work, via any means: print, graphic, sculpture, multimedia, audio, or other medium. We support the right of humans to control their artistic ability.

The scanning, uploading, and distribution of this book without permission is a theft of the author's intellectual property. Thank you for your support of the author's rights.

Editing, design, distribution by Bublish
Published by Do Good Media

ISBN: 979-8-9938161-0-4 (paperback)
ISBN: 979-8-9938161-1-1 (hardcover)
ISBN: 979-8-9938161-2-8 (eBook)

www.marciadawood.com

PRAISE FOR UNAPOLOGETIC WEALTH

"Everyone has a story about money, but few ever stop to examine it. Unapologetic Wealth is a guide to becoming the most empowered version of yourself. Marcia Dawood reminds us that real wealth begins within."

Anthony Scaramucci, Managing Partner, SkyBridge

"Marcia Dawood's Unapologetic Wealth reminds us that our relationship with money shapes far more than our finances. It influences how we live, give, and grow across a lifetime. This book will inspire readers to live with meaning and build a legacy that lasts".

Dr. Kerry Burnight, NYT Best-selling Author, JOYSPAN: The Art and Science of Thriving in Life's Second Half

"Unapologetic Wealth is, without doubt, an essential must-read for any woman who's ready to be financially empowered. With clarity, warmth, and deep wisdom, Marcia Dawood helps women heal the conditioning that holds them back and step into a new, liberated relationship with money."

Barbara Huson, author of Overcoming Underearning and Rewire for Wealth

"Marcia Dawood understands how essential it is to take control of your financial life, even when it feels daunting. Unapologetic Wealth is a wise and compassionate guide to doing just that, and to building a future on your own terms."

Dorie Clark, Wall Street Journal & USA Today bestselling author of The Long Game

"Women thrive when they have both health and wealth. Unapologetic Wealth gives women the tools to build financial strength with the same intention we bring to our well-being. Marcia Dawood has created a powerful guide for lasting impact."

Dr. Brittany Barreto, Author of Unlocking Women's Health

For those who came before us, who worked, sacrificed, and persevered so that we could stand taller today.

&

For the next generation, who deserve to inherit a world where wealth, power, and possibility are equally shared, and who will carry this progress even further.

TABLE OF CONTENTS

Praise for Unapologetic Wealth iii
Introduction ix
Chapter One: If Money Feels Weird, You Are Not Alone 1
Chapter Two: Generational Welts: Money Beliefs Passed
                Down Through Silence..23
Chapter Three: The Quiet Grip of Money Guilt 41
Chapter Four: The Ripple Effect of Playing Small 64
Chapter Five: Shift from Playing Small to Being Bold.............88
Chapter Six: Honor the Past, Reshape the Future................107
Chapter Seven: Live Financial Fluidity 125
Chapter Eight: Redefine Wealth..135
Chapter Nine: Use Money Intentionally 151
Chapter Ten: Put It All into Practice 168

Closing Thoughts: Live Your Legacy Now 175
Author's Note 183
Resources 185
Acknowledgments 187
Author Bio 189
References 191

INTRODUCTION

I magine waking up in the morning and the first thing you feel is *ease*.

Not the jolt of panic, not the mental math of bills and deadlines, and not the needs and expectations placed on you today. Just a quiet steadiness in your chest.

You can take a breath instead of grinding through yet another day.

You can say yes to the trip, the time off, the idea that has been tugging at you for years.

You can walk away from what weighs you down.

You can invest in what lights you up.

You can give openly to people, to causes, to your own future.

That's what wealth can do. Not just the numbers-in-an-account kind of wealth, but the grounded, intentional, deeply personal kind. The kind that also includes:

- Relationship wealth
- Time wealth
- Health wealth
- Creative wealth
- Knowledge wealth

Many women are doing the work; they are earning, saving, giving, and supporting those around them, and yet they still feel stuck. Not because they are doing something wrong, but because they have been given a set of rules, beliefs, and expectations that are long outdated. In addition to limiting financial decisions, these rules also influence other aspects of life: how we use our time, how we use our voice, and how we care for ourselves.

Maybe you have felt a quiet second-guessing. A voice that says, *You should know more by now.* Or *you don't really belong in this room.* Or *wanting more is greedy, selfish, or … not for you.*

I've felt it too. And I know it doesn't have to be this way.

Unapologetic Wealth isn't about chasing someone else's version of success. It's about recognizing your own financial power and the power within to create a life you love. It's about unlearning the guilt, the fear, and the beliefs you didn't choose but probably inherited. And it's about building something solid enough to support not only your needs, but also your boldest dreams.

This book explores how to reframe our relationship with money so that is no longer something we fear, avoid, or hand off to someone else. And for that to happen, we must begin at the root—not only with strategy but also with mindset.

Mindset shapes our experience with everything. It's the filter we apply to money, risk, ambition, security, and more. It influences how we save, spend, and invest—or don't. For women especially, mindset has often been shaped by exclusion, silence, and inherited narratives that limit what we believe is possible.

Our mindset is our foundation. The good news is that it's not fixed; it can evolve. It's like fear that softens when we talk about things—when we name the unknown, lay out the options, and start to visualize a path forward. Fear causes people to avoid difficult conversations or dentist visits because they are afraid of bad news. When they finally do the thing, they realize their outcome is at least better than expected, even mostly good. The anxiety was worse than the reality.

Our mindset about money works in the same way. The fear of looking too closely can keep us stuck. But once we overcome

Introduction

the fear, once we begin to understand it and talk about it, our mindset shifts, and everything starts to feel more possible.

That's what this book is about—reframing how we think about money so we can stop fearing it, start talking about it, and start using it to reflect who we are and what we care about. At its core, money is simply paper with ink or numbers on a screen. We are the ones who give it meaning, power, and emotional significance. I've seen firsthand how powerful a shift in mindset about money can be. And I've also observed that many people, especially women, do not feel they're allowed to make that shift at all.

Women are often told to be responsible with money but not to take real ownership of it. When it comes to building wealth, we're expected to manage day-to-day finances, stick to a budget, or stretch a dollar, but not necessarily to think big, invest boldly, or believe we deserve more. There is often an unspoken expectation that we'll step up financially for others: covering family expenses, helping a partner through a tough stretch, or stepping in for parents or siblings. We quietly fulfill these expectations without recognition. But when it comes to investing in ourselves, growing our assets, or making bold financial decisions, encouragement is hushed, if it exists at all. A cultural undercurrent still suggests that men should assume financial leadership, while women should be cautious rather than bold. This message may not be spoken aloud, but it's absorbed over time and holds many women back.

On top of that, money remains largely a taboo subject. We are not supposed to talk about it at the dinner table or even with friends. We avoid conversations about salaries, debt, savings, or investments because we are afraid of being judged, misunderstood, or exposed. Most people, regardless of income, still aren't given the space to explore what a healthy relationship with money looks like. It's not just that we weren't taught how to invest or plan financially; we weren't even encouraged to ask questions. So, money has become emotionally charged, closely tied to self-worth, shame, comparison, and fear. As a result, too many people remain silent and stuck.

In *The Psychology of Money*, Morgan Housel writes, "Your personal experiences with money make up maybe 0.00000000001 percent of what's happened in the world, but maybe 80 percent of how you think the world works." This line says so much. Most of us don't realize how limited our financial worldview truly is. We form beliefs based on what we have seen, how we have lived, and what we have been told—often during childhood, sometimes in crisis, but rarely with a complete picture. If you grew up in a household where money was tight, you might see it as something scarce and stressful. If your family never talked about money, you might view it as something taboo or off-limits. If you only ever saw money being used for power or control, you might feel uneasy associating it with anything positive.

These early experiences shape our mindset, influencing how we respond to raises, emergency expenses, retirement discussions, or significant purchases. They determine whether we perceive opportunity or risk and whether we believe wealth is attainable or reserved for "other people." Yet all of this is based on a narrow slice of reality—*our* reality, not the full spectrum of what's possible. We act on assumptions we have never questioned, often oblivious to their accuracy.

That's why shifting our mindset is so important. It helps us pause and ask, *Is this belief true, or just familiar? Is this my voice or someone else's?* Because until we name what we believe, we can't change it. And if we want to use money differently—to build freedom, to create impact, to invest in our values—we must think differently first.

For women in particular, their beliefs have been shaped by a system that excluded them for centuries. It is only since World War II that women have entered the workforce in significant numbers. For the first time in history, women are not just earning—they are accumulating wealth. According to Bloomberg,

Introduction

by 2030, they are expected to control up to $34 trillion in U.S. financial assets.

But access alone doesn't guarantee action. Without action, that wealth will not achieve its full potential.

This book explores how to close that gap and embrace *financial fluidity*—a mindset and strategy for aligning your money with your values, goals, and life. Throughout this book, I will explain what this means and why it matters now more than ever.

We will discuss how your voice and financial choices hold power.

After reading this book, you will gain the clarity needed to develop your own personal financial philosophy. It will help you navigate money, risk, and wealth at any level, enabling you to create a life and impact that genuinely reflect what matters most to you.

For me, this is personal.

I grew up with parents who encouraged me to pursue any path I wanted, yet there were unspoken limits. Boys had "boy jobs," and girls had "girl jobs." I excelled at mathematics, but no one ever suggested finance as a career option. I wonder how different my life might have been if they had.

Decades later, I still observe how such quiet constraints echo through women's lives. For centuries, women have been cast as caregivers and supporters, while men occupied roles associated with power and wealth. Over time, this division solidified into prevailing beliefs: play small, remain invisible, and keep others comfortable.

When women break those rules by leading boldly or speaking directly, they are often labeled as aggressive. The problem is not with women, nor is it with men. The real issue lies in the centuries-old narratives we have all inherited.

While women have made incredible strides, the journey remains challenging. Many balance careers, families, and high expectations, leaving little energy to change the narrative. It often feels safer to adhere to familiar patterns than to challenge them.

But I believe in a different future. A world where women's and men's perspectives equally influence decisions, where ambition and generosity go hand in hand, and where wealth serves as a tool for change rather than a measure of worth.

That kind of change begins with awareness. When women recognize their inherited limitations for what they truly are, merely old stories, they can choose to create new narratives. And when they do, the ripple effects extend to future generations.

That's what this book aims to ignite: not just movement, but *a* movement away from limits and toward unapologetic wealth.

Chapter One

If Money Feels Weird, You Are Not Alone

Money. Why does it feel complicated? Be sensible. Don't be greedy. Don't talk about money. Don't want too much, and don't have too little. And definitely don't flaunt it if you do have it. These are messages many of us have absorbed throughout our lives.

You are smart, hardworking, and responsible. Perhaps you already earn a good income, or maybe you want to earn more.

No matter where you are right now, why, after spending time earning, saving, and doing your best (or trying to), does it still feel like there's a layer of discomfort or disconnect you can't shake when it comes to finances? Even if you have systems in place or people helping you, why do you sometimes feel uncertain about what you are supposed to do with your money?

Money is a complex subject. You have tried to make practical decisions, followed advice, and avoided reckless mistakes. You have budgeted, saved when possible, and worked hard to build some stability, even if debt remains part of the picture. Maybe you even have a financial advisor or a partner who "takes care of the money stuff." Yet, somewhere beneath it all, there is still a quiet feeling that you are not truly in control of your financial life—that you are orbiting it rather than owning it.

If any of that sounds familiar, you are not alone.

Before we move on, let's take a moment to check in. Reflect on where you believe you are right now and consider any changes you'd like to see in your financial situation or in your life overall. This will serve as your baseline. Later, at the end of the book, you'll do a similar exercise to assess whether your perspective has changed after reading and engaging with the exercises and reflections at the end of each chapter. Having this starting point makes your progress visible and reminds you that even small shifts add up.

As you work through the exercises and questions, you may notice patterns, strengths, or areas that feel ready for change. Whatever comes to mind, let it land and trust that this is the first step toward something better.

Quick Check-in

Find a comfortable seat and take a few deep, cleansing breaths.

Then answer these questions without censoring, judgment, or criticism. Simply write (or think through, if you're not in a good place to write) whatever comes to mind.

List three things that characterize your current financial or life situation. (These may be positive, negative, or neutral.)

_____

_____

_____

If Money Feels Weird, You Are Not Alone

List three things you would like to change about your current financial or life situation.

_____

_____

_____

So many people, especially women, feel disconnected from their money, not because they are incapable or uninterested, but because something deeper stands in the way. They often believe they need more information, better tools, or a clearer plan. And sometimes this is true. But more often, what truly holds them back are harder-to-identify factors: limiting beliefs rooted in the past and feelings of money guilt.

Limiting beliefs, such as "I'm not good with money" or "It's selfish to want more," often run so deep that we don't even recognize them as beliefs. They feel like truths. However, most of them were shaped by generations that didn't have the same opportunities we have today. We have internalized caution as wisdom and self-denial as virtue. While these lessons may have been necessary in the past, they no longer serve us well today.

We stand at a cultural crossroads where the scarcity-based beliefs we inherited meet the opportunities for abundance now within our reach. On one side are the women who came before us, those who had to focus on survival. On the other is a world where we can build wealth boldly and on our own terms. And yet many of us still carry the emotional weight of the past. If we don't shift this mindset, we risk passing it down, even as the world around us changes. It is our responsibility to break this cycle, not only for ourselves but for the generations that follow. If we remain stuck in inherited fear and limitation, we are not only holding ourselves back; we are also passing that burden on to our daughters.

Another factor holding us back is money guilt. This is not the obvious kind of guilt, like doing something morally wrong or even eating an entire bucket of ice cream. Rather, it is a quieter, more persistent guilt—the kind that shows up when you feel bad spending on yourself, even when you can afford it. When you downplay what you've earned, when you feel selfish for wanting more, or irresponsible for spending too freely. When you tell yourself you should already know how this works and feel ashamed that you don't.

This guilt isn't about logic—it's about legacy. It is passed down from previous generations, much like the limiting beliefs shaped by those same generations. Over time, these messages become part of your mindset, influencing your behavior. They show up in the way you make decisions, set goals, and define what is enough. They keep you cautious when you want to be bold. Hesitant when you want to be intentional. Safe when you are ready to grow.

This book is here to challenge all of that and explore ways to change it.

Unapologetic Wealth is about more than dollars and cents; it is about what we tell ourselves about money every day. This goes beyond simply managing your money and leans into understanding your feelings to make better financial decisions. It's about the stories you've been told and the ones you've picked up along the way. Some of them begin in childhood, shaped by messages about what is enough, who has money and who doesn't, and what is considered good when it comes to spending or saving. Others may have taken root later—in workplaces that paid you less than you deserved, in relationships where you deferred financial control, or in moments when you doubted your own instincts and let someone else decide what was best for you. Over time, these stories compound. They shape how you think, how you spend, how you save, and, most importantly, how you see yourself in relation to money.

Sometimes, there are events you can't plan for, such as the sudden loss of a job, the end of a marriage, or the death of a loved one. Circumstances like these can shift your financial reality overnight, no matter how careful or prepared you have been. In such moments, it becomes even more important to understand not only the numbers but also the beliefs that guide your responses to life changes.

Overall, you might believe you are being practical or responsible with money when, in reality, you are playing small out of habit. You might think you are simply "not a money person," when, in fact, you have never been given the framework or permission to define what a healthy, empowered relationship with money looks like on your own terms.

Imagine rewriting the stories you've been told, including perhaps the ones you've told yourself. Imagine claiming ownership not just over your financial decisions but over the beliefs that often unconsciously drive them. You will learn to think about money in a way that aligns with your values and vision, rather than being shaped by guilt, fear, or outdated expectations.

When your mindset shifts, your choices shift. You stop making decisions out of caution and start making them with clarity. You stop seeing money as something to fear, hoard, or downplay and start seeing it as a tool for expression, alignment, and agency.

That's the essence of unapologetic wealth—not just possessing money but using it intentionally and confidently to shape your life on your own terms.

I know this matters, not just because I have studied it but because I have lived it, questioned it, and navigated through it myself.

I began to recognize this disconnect from money decisions as part of a larger pattern when I was unexpectedly introduced to a world I had thought was reserved for others. In 2012, while living in Pittsburgh, PA, I was invited to an angel investing meeting. I had no understanding of what angel investing was, and had never been exposed to discussions about money and investing in this way before. That evening, I met several local entrepreneurs working on bold, innovative start-ups, and I was immediately intrigued. I learned that angel investing involves individuals investing their own money in early-stage companies, often providing both capital and mentorship to help them grow.

Over the next twelve years, I learned everything about the world of early-stage investing and how it operates. Initially, I assumed this space was reserved for the ultra-wealthy and well-connected, much like what is portrayed on TV. However, it doesn't matter whether you have a lot of money or very little to get started. Those who want to invest for change can do so in numerous ways by making investments in private, early-stage companies aligned with their values. For me, that change is deeply personal. After losing my mother to amyotrophic lateral sclerosis (ALS, also known as Lou Gehrig's disease) in 2018, I became deeply committed to supporting solutions that advance research and innovation in areas like this devastating disease. Investing became not only a financial endeavor but also a way to honor her memory and contribute to something greater than myself.

In 2021, I set out on a quest to demystify the early-stage investing space by launching *The Angel Next Door* podcast. My aim was to highlight everyday individuals who are investing to drive change. This could be anyone, even your next-door neighbor. Since then, the podcast has evolved to cover a variety of topics, including different ways to invest, the reasons behind people's investment decisions, and insights from U.S. Congress members. As of this writing, the podcast has more than 150 episodes. As a member and chair of the Small Business Capital Formation Advisory Committee to the U.S. Securities and Exchange Commission, I have had the opportunity to feature a few SEC commissioners to hear their take on entrepreneurship as well. In addition to the podcast, I spoke at TEDxCharlotte in 2022 and later released

If Money Feels Weird, You Are Not Alone

the book *Do Good While Doing Well: Invest for Change, Reap Financial Rewards, and Increase Your Happiness* along with an accompanying workbook in 2024, all in an effort to make investing for change more accessible.

Over the years, when I spoke to people about investing, their reactions were mixed. Some were curious but cautious, while others flat-out said it felt too risky. However, the most common response I heard was, "I don't even know how investing of any kind fits into my financial life." Many believed they were bad with money, and some mentioned that their husbands handled everything. We need more people, especially women, to recognize that investing can be a powerful tool not only for building potential wealth but also for shaping the kind of world we want to live in.

This book builds on the philosophy behind *Do Good While Doing Well*, but it also takes a step back to examine the bigger picture. Instead of focusing solely on how to invest for change, we explore something more foundational: your relationship with money. The habits. The stories you've inherited or internalized about what money means, what you're permitted to do with it, and whether you're "good" at managing it. Before you can confidently invest in companies or causes that matter to you, you must first believe you are capable of making those decisions. That belief begins with mindset.

Money trauma refers to the old stories, past experiences, and deeply rooted emotional patterns that quietly shape how we relate to money. It's not always obvious. Sometimes it's subtle—a parent stressing over bills, a divorce that left you financially vulnerable, a situation where you stayed quiet about money to appear likable. But it stays with us. It shapes our beliefs, habits, and perceptions of what is possible.

With that insight, I realized that before we could invest with intention or build wealth unapologetically, we needed something else: a new kind of relationship with money. One rooted in clarity, compassion, and confidence, rather than shame or scarcity.

This is not a personal finance manual in the traditional sense. You won't find stock-picking strategies, quick ways to get rich, or rigid formulas for "doing money right." Instead, this book focuses on examining what you already have and shifting your mindset about it, regardless of your income or bank balance. Whether you're just starting out or decades into your career, this book is relevant. It is the book I wish I had in my twenties, but it is equally powerful for women in midlife and beyond who are ready to see money differently. When your mindset shifts, you can align your life and finances so that every choice moves you closer to the life you want to live. To create a life you love at all stages.

My Own Money Journey

I have always considered myself an optimistic person. I tend to see the glass as half full, or at least refillable. But then I met my husband, Izzy, and I realized there is a whole other level of optimism. His optimism made mine look like a cautious suggestion.

Early in our relationship, I'd bring up something I was stressed about: a situation at work, a family issue, or one of those vague "what if everything goes sideways" ideas in my head. I'd be deep into it, laying out every angle and building a worst-case scenario as if it were my part-time job.

He'd listen patiently, nodding like a therapist in a romantic comedy, and then, without fail, he'd hit me with the same question:

"So . . . what's the worst that can happen?"

At first, I found this kind of annoying. I had just spent ten minutes building a perfectly good panic, and he wanted me to *rationally* deconstruct it?

Still, we'd go through it.

"Well," I'd say, "if this project doesn't go well, my boss will be upset."

"And?"

"Then maybe I'll be seen as unreliable."

"Okay. Then what?"

"Then . . . maybe I'll get fired, burn through my savings, and end up living under a bridge eating the stale granola bars I found in the bottom of my bag."

He never laughed at me, but he did raise an eyebrow. "Okay," he'd say. "And how likely is that?"

We'd walk through the whole chain of events, scenario by scenario. It didn't magically erase the worry, but it gave it structure. Once I could see the edges of the unknown, it didn't feel so bottomless. I wasn't spiraling anymore. I was thinking.

His approach made me realize how powerful it is to name the fear, say it out loud, and face it directly. Doing so takes away its grip. We didn't have a word for it then, but now I understand what we were doing: shifting our mindset. Quietly, consistently, and over time, it began to change how I navigated uncertainty—not just in life, but especially regarding financial matters. Izzy's optimism was constructive and well-defined. He made space for possibility while staying grounded. That mindset helped us stay clear, focused, and able to move forward with confidence, even in uncertainty.

Izzy brought a refreshing perspective on money. He came to the U.S. for college on a tennis scholarship with little more than the clothes on his back. As an immigrant, he never took opportunity for granted. He was smart and focused, landed an entry-level finance job after school, and steadily worked his way up. But what stood out most wasn't his career path; it was his mindset about money. To him, money was just a tool. Useful, important, but not a measure of personal worth.

I grew up in a modest household. One of the greatest gifts my dad gave me was his openness about money. He kept the bills in an old shoebox, and on payday, he'd carry it to the kitchen table like clockwork. I was probably eight or nine years old when he started asking me to sit with him during this task. I'd watch as he opened the box, spread out the envelopes, and explained what was due and why. It wasn't fancy, but it was transparent.

He taught me that, regardless of your income level or the stage of life, you can make the most of what you have. Living within your means was the goal, no matter what those means looked like.

I remember how practical he was about major purchases, especially cars. Safety mattered; status didn't. A car was meant to get you where you needed to go, not to impress anyone. I have carried that mindset forward to my stepsons. For a while, my car had a chip in the windshield; it wasn't large enough to block my vision, but it was noticeable. My oldest stepson asked why I hadn't gotten it fixed right away. I told him, "Because there are other priorities." I had learned that not everything needs to be fixed the moment it breaks, especially if it isn't affecting my life in a meaningful way. I don't think I ever repaired that chip until years later, when we sold the car. Maybe you had someone in your life who passed down money lessons, or maybe this is less familiar to you. Either way, the truth is that the real value isn't in the things we own but in how we choose to live.

During the early stages of my career in education, I worked with students doing everything they could to move forward. Every day, I saw what resilience looked like, and it gave me a deep sense of gratitude for what I had. At the same time, I had friends working in industries where wealth was front and center, and the lifestyle was different. Their lives revolved around keeping up appearances, purchasing large houses, and driving expensive cars. That contrast stuck with me.

In addition to my dad's lessons about living within my means, I learned to save diligently and avoid unnecessary risks. The message was clear: Play it safe. Protect what you have. Don't reach too far. For a long time, I practiced that mindset. I took pride in being careful and responsible, believing that's what it meant to be "good" with money. Yet beneath that sense of responsibility, I felt a quiet guilt—an unspoken pressure not to show off what I had, not to ask for too much, and not to act as if I deserved more than I received. I stayed small without even realizing it. Early in my career, I didn't negotiate as hard as I could have. I didn't push for bigger opportunities when I started my first job out of college. Instead, I chose a retail buying position where many of my peers were. Overall, I made safe, sensible choices, staying away from bold ones.

But when I married Izzy, my perspective began to shift. Izzy approached money with a different energy—one of openness, possibility, and trust in opportunity. His approach was expansive, not reckless. He could evaluate a financial decision by considering what it might create, not just what it would cost. Being around him showed me that living within your means doesn't have to equate to shrinking your life. It's about understanding your current reality while still leaving room for growth, investment, and joy. I started noticing it in small ways. When I might hesitate to spend money on a weekend trip because it felt unnecessary, Izzy would tell me to book it without guilt, seeing it as a chance to create memories, deepen relationships, and recharge. He factored in the cost but also weighed the return—connection, joy, energy. That changed something in me. I began to realize that financial responsibility isn't about cutting everything down to the lowest number; it's about choosing what's worth expanding for.

There were times when our means and goals didn't align perfectly. Instead of retreating into fear, I learned to ask better questions: What is needed now? What is needed soon? What can we responsibly plan for later?

Letting go of my tight grip on money didn't make me less responsible; it made me freer. Free to make decisions that aligned with my values. Free to invest in opportunities that mattered to me. Free to live fully in the present while still preparing for the future. I call this mindset financial fluidity.

Financial fluidity is a flexible and responsive approach to managing money. It's about creating a relationship with your finances that is strong enough to support you but flexible enough to evolve with you. It moves you beyond rigid rules and limiting beliefs, allowing you to adjust as your life changes—whether you are experiencing growth, loss, transition, or new opportunities.

Because life isn't linear, your money story won't be either. And that's perfectly okay. In fact, that's the whole point.

Financial fluidity gives you the freedom to honor your past, live fully in your present, and invest wisely in your future. All while staying aligned with who you are and the life you are building.

At this point, you might be thinking, *Okay . . . I agree that money can be complicated.* It's not just dollars and decisions. It's memories, emotions, fears, hopes, all tangled up together.

If you've ever felt the urge to downplay what you have, questioned whether you deserve more, or wondered if it's even okay to want a different financial life, you are not alone.

The truth is most of us didn't just wake up one day with money guilt. We picked it up slowly over time—from our families, from society, and from the unspoken rules we were expected to follow. It has been woven into how we think, how we talk (or don't talk) about money, and how we determine what's possible for ourselves.

Before we can move forward and build a financial life that feels free, aligned, and unapologetic, we must first understand more about money mindset, the root of its cause, and how it has shaped us.

Defining Quiet Money Guilt

Quiet money guilt shows up as hesitation, hiding, minimizing yourself, or playing small, even when no one else asks you to. It can influence your personal choices as well as broader aspects of life. Money guilt patterns can operate in subtle ways that you might not even notice. These patterns can also create rifts even in the strongest relationships. Take sisters Gwen and Gina as an example. They grew up in a rural neighborhood in a family that emphasized working hard, being polite, and not asking for too much. As kids, they were close, sharing clothes, whispering in the dark, and always knowing what the other was thinking.

They both did well in school, went off to reputable colleges, and believed that if they followed the rules and made smart choices, life would reward them in kind.

After graduation, their lives began to look quite different. Gwen secured an entry-level position with great potential at a well-known company. She stayed late, took on extra responsibilities, and made herself indispensable. Over time, she advanced, first into a team lead role, then into management. She married a few years later, had children, and managed to maintain her career throughout it all. It wasn't easy, but it aligned with how she wanted to live her life.

Gina's story wasn't quite as smooth. She got married shortly after college and had a baby within the year. She tried to start a career, but with a newborn and limited childcare options, it felt like running uphill through mud. Eventually, she let go of the idea of a traditional job and began working at home babysitting other kids to help with expenses. It was flexible and practical, but it never really felt like a career—not like the life she had hoped for.

As the years passed, the once easy closeness between the sisters started to stretch and thin. There was no falling out. No big argument. Just a quiet drift.

When Gwen got promoted, she didn't mention it during their calls. It wasn't that she thought Gina would be angry; she simply didn't want to make her feel worse. So, she kept the conversation light, talking about the kids, the weather, and other safe topics.

Gina noticed Gwen's new house on social media—the kitchen remodel, the summer vacations, the way everything seemed settled. She never said anything, but a knot tightened in her chest every time she scrolled past another photo. It wasn't rage. It wasn't even envy, not exactly. Just a gnawing feeling she couldn't name. Like she'd missed something. Like Gwen had taken a path she wasn't able to take.

She had chosen her life. She loved her family, and her husband did well. But still, part of her wondered how things could have turned out only if she had made bolder choices, like Gwen.

And yet, neither of them ever talked about any of it: not the tension, not the shame, not the quiet resentments. Because in their world, as in so many others, money simply wasn't something you discussed. Not with family, not with friends, not even with yourself.

This is what money guilt looks like. It doesn't always scream. Sometimes it just lingers—beneath the silence, behind the small talk, between the lines of a conversation that once felt easy.

Gwen holds back because she doesn't want to make Gina feel bad. Gina shrinks because she's already burdened by the feeling that she hasn't achieved enough.

How Did We Get Here?

Understanding our relationship with money and value requires us to step back and see the bigger picture. To understand why so many women feel disconnected from their money, we need to look to the past. The financial disconnection many women experience today stems from centuries of systemic exclusion. This history has shaped patterns of thinking that we are still trying to break free from. Throughout most of human history, women's relationship with money has been controlled by marriage and family roles rather than independent economic activity.

From ancient dowry systems, initially designed as financial protection for women but later used as wealth transfers controlled by men, to the nineteenth century's coverture laws giving husbands complete control over their wives' property, women have been systematically excluded from financial systems. Even when women possessed wealth, it typically came through marriage negotiations rather than independent financial activity. This all reinforced the idea that financial matters were outside women's domain.

This financial exclusion persisted well into modern history. As late as the 1960s, women in the U.S. couldn't open bank accounts without a male cosigner. Until 1974, banks routinely denied women credit cards and loans solely because of their gender.[i] A female friend told me that in 1993, a bank asked her to have her father cosign a mortgage, even though she had the necessary income and down payment to qualify for the loan.

Our female ancestors fought for the basic financial rights we now take for granted: the right to own property, keep our own wages, enter contracts, and build independent credit histories. This liberation is only a few generations old, if that, which is a mere blink of an eye in the grand scope of history. The exclusion of earlier generations has left a lasting impact. Today, many women still struggle with financial confidence and harbor inherited limiting beliefs that money management is neither their responsibility nor within their capabilities. Changing women's relationship with money isn't just about learning financial skills; it requires dismantling deeply ingrained beliefs shaped by centuries of exclusion. By acknowledging this legacy, women can begin the journey toward financial empowerment with compassion for themselves and appreciation for how far they have come in such a short time.

The Great Wealth Transfer

This point in history presents an unprecedented opportunity for women to reshape financial systems. According to Bloomberg, by 2030, women are expected to control approximately 38 percent of the United States' investable assets—nearly $34 trillion. This represents a significant increase from the $7.3 trillion controlled by women in the mid-2010s.

Demographics primarily drive this shift. Women typically outlive men by five to ten years and often marry partners who are approximately two years older.[ii] These factors make women more likely to inherit and subsequently manage family assets for extended periods.

However, this isn't just about inheritance. Women are increasingly generating their own wealth through career advancement, entrepreneurship, and investment. They are starting businesses at higher rates than men and are more likely to engage in impact-driven investing, allocating money toward businesses as well as causes that align with their values.[iii]

Despite their growing financial power, women still struggle with confidence in money management and financial growth. Research shows that only 25 percent of affluent women feel comfortable making investment decisions independently, 15 percent fewer than men. This confidence gap persists even though studies suggest that women's investment strategies often yield better long-term outcomes.[iv]

Women Aren't the Only People Struggling

I wrote this book primarily for women. However, as I spoke to people about investing, I met many men who also experienced a sense of financial disconnection. Many people perceive money as something separate from themselves—intimidating, overwhelming, or beyond their control. This often comes from financial decisions they have postponed or that others made for them, leaving them feeling powerless and disconnected from their finances. For some, a life-changing event forced them to confront their financial reality directly. Many were taught to be responsible with money but were never empowered to take full ownership of their financial decisions. Even those seeking greater confidence, engagement, and control over their wealth often feel unsure about where to start or who to ask. Money can be a taboo topic for many, and the less it is discussed, the deeper the cycle of disconnection becomes.

And for many women, myself included, money isn't just a solo journey. It's something we navigate in partnership, which naturally brings different perspectives to the table. When I married Izzy, I was introduced to his view that money is simply a tool, not a source of stress or a measure of worth. Over time, that perspective began to shift something in me.

But that shift didn't happen in isolation. It took place through conversations, shared decisions, and moments of working things out together. Like many couples, we came into the relationship with different upbringings, spending habits, and comfort levels regarding money. At times, our perspectives clashed, but there were also moments of alignment and learning. That's what partnership looks like: not perfect agreement, but mutual respect and a willingness to stay in dialogue.

Being in a financial partnership means checking in regularly, yes, with numbers, but also on goals, values, and changes in your lives. It means being open about fears without letting them drive every decision. It also requires learning to view each other's approaches not as better or worse, but as reflections of what has shaped you. When both partners feel heard and empowered, money becomes what it was always meant to be: a shared resource for building the life you both desire.

This kind of active engagement is more important than ever as pensions are becoming a thing of the past. According to the Federal Reserve Bank of St. Louis, in 1980, about 38 percent of private-sector employees had a defined benefit pension. By 2025, that number had dropped to just 11 percent.[v] Fewer people can rely on a guaranteed income in retirement, which means the responsibility for long-term financial security now rests more heavily on individuals and families. Ownership, partnership, and clarity around money are essential.

Redefining Wealth

One of the most fundamental shifts this book aims to address is the redefinition of wealth. Too often, people equate their self-worth with their income or bank account balance, regardless of whether that income comes from a job, a business, or any other source. They pursue bigger paychecks, higher revenue, or more clients, assuming that more money will bring more freedom. But what often happens is the opposite. As their income grows, so do their expenses. They upgrade their lifestyle, take on more debt, and add more obligations, until they are working harder than ever just to maintain a version of success that doesn't actually bring them peace, joy, or security.

That's not financial freedom; it's financial strain in disguise.

Chris was an executive who, by all appearances, had made it. He held a prestigious position, earned a generous income, and enjoyed a life of travel and luxury. But beneath the surface, he had no savings, his credit cards were maxed out, and the lifestyle offered no financial safety net. When new leadership arrived at his company, he was forced to choose between a severance package that wouldn't last and a demotion with lower pay. He accepted the demotion and grew increasingly miserable. After four decades at the company, he was laid off. Years earlier, he had been advised to reduce the family's discretionary spending if he wanted a comfortable retirement. However, scaling back wasn't easy, especially since his wife was reluctant to give up the lifestyle they were used to. The dinners out, the travel, the image—all of it had become part of their identity. Despite a lifetime of hard work and high earnings, they found themselves financially strained and deeply stressed.

Their story serves as a reminder that income without flexibility can leave a family vulnerable. A big paycheck doesn't create freedom if every dollar is already spoken for. Real security comes from being able to adapt, adjust, scale back, or move forward without everything collapsing. This is the essence of financial fluidity. Financial fluidity is about using money as a tool, not just to chase financial goals but to design a life that reflects your values. It's about making intentional choices, not reactive ones. It's about having the flexibility to adapt to life's changes, whether that means scaling back, stepping forward, or pausing altogether. It's not about getting everything right;

it's about building a foundation strong enough to support what matters to you through all seasons of change.

Financial fluidity goes beyond dollars and cents. It also shows up in how we relate to each other. Money can quietly shape relationships, creating distance through guilt, comparison, or unspoken expectations. Approaching money with openness and adaptability has the power to transform not only our finances but also our connections, as seen in Gwen and Gina's story. After years of silent tension, an argument finally brought their unspoken feelings about money into the open. It wasn't easy; tears, anger, and years of comparison and guilt spilled into the conversation. But for the first time, they truly heard each other. They recognized how guilt and unspoken assumptions had built walls between them. From that raw, messy interaction, something new began to grow—honesty, understanding, and healing. Slowly, they began to rebuild the sisterhood they once shared—this time on a foundation that allowed them to discuss money, success, struggles, and dreams more openly and without judgment. Sometimes, healing begins simply by naming what has been there all along.

We need to talk about money more often, openly, honestly, and without shame. Whether it's between sisters, friends, partners, or even just quietly with ourselves, discussing money breaks the isolation that guilt and fear thrive on. These conversations create space for healing. They help us recognize patterns we didn't even realize were shaping our lives. They help us understand that the burden we've been carrying isn't a personal failure — it's unexamined history. And once we see it, we can begin to change it.

Without reflection, it's easy to believe that financial growth alone can heal what lies beneath. But too often, the pursuit of more only deepens the sense of disconnection. How many times have we seen people who, as they earn more, simply acquire more—bigger homes, luxury cars, and expensive jewelry—all to *look* wealthy? But are they truly wealthy? There is a difference between being rich and being wealthy.

Personally, I don't love the word *rich*. It feels narrow and transactional, tied only to a number in a bank account. You can be rich in dollars and still feel disconnected, anxious, or alone. *Wealth*, on the other hand, is expansive. True wealth includes your finances, yes, but also your time, your health, your relationships, and your sense of purpose. Wealth is about choice. It's about living with intention, not obligation. It's about being able to say yes to the things that matter and no to the things that don't.

This book is designed to help you move toward true wealth. To get there, we'll walk through a process that helps you understand how you got here, shift what no longer serves you, and build something stronger in its place.

This transformation, from financial anxiety to financial fluidity, from money guilt to unapologetic wealth, is what this book is designed to help you achieve. But like any meaningful change, it requires a roadmap.

Chapters two through four will examine the roots of the financial disconnect many women feel. We will look at the cultural, historical, and systemic factors that helped shape this mindset so you can understand that it didn't start with you and is not your fault.

Chapters five through seven will focus on how to begin making meaningful changes. We'll discuss about how to identify limiting beliefs, reclaim your agency, and take action in ways that build genuine, sustainable confidence—whether you are managing, earning, spending, or investing money.

Chapters eight through the end will bring everything together. You'll develop your own personal financial philosophy—a grounded, values-driven framework that will guide your decisions and shape your long-term relationship with money.

Along the way, you'll find exercises, reflection questions, and tools designed to help you integrate what you are learning in real time. Some people enjoy doing exercises, while others don't—and that's perfectly okay. Even if you think they are not for you, try a few anyway. You might be surprised by what comes up. The shift begins in these moments of pause, where insight transforms into action. You don't need to have perfect answers, just honest ones. Approach this process with curiosity. Trust that each time you take a deeper look inward, you move closer to a financial life that's truly your own.

The money story you have inherited doesn't have to be the one you keep living. You have the power to create a new story.

You have the power to shape your financial future. And it starts here.

Reflection Questions

For each reflection question, write your answers in the space provided, use your own journal, or simply sit quietly and think them through. There is no single right way. Choose the method that feels most comfortable. What matters is taking a few honest moments to pause, reflect, and truly listen to your own thoughts.

What is your earliest memory involving money?

_____

_____

_____

_____

How do you currently define *being good with money*? Where did this definition come from?

_____

_____

_____

_____

Exercise: How You Handle Money

For this exercise, write directly in the book or put down your answers in a journal.

On a scale of 1–10 (10 being very comfortable and 1 being not uncomfortable):
How comfortable are you with:

- Handling the household finances (paying bills, budgeting, shopping for necessities)?
- Saving versus spending? Do you have a monthly plan outlining how much gets saved and what can be spent on discretionary items?
- Investing? Do you have any investments? Do you make the decisions yourself or with a partner or advisor?

HOW YOU HANDLE MONEY

RATE YOURSELF BETWEEN 1 AND 10 WITH HOW COMFORTABLE YOU ARE IN EACH CATEGORY

HOUSEHOLD FINANCES

1 2 3 4 5 6 7 8 9 10

NOT COMFORTABLE   VERY COMFORTABLE

SAVING/SPENDING

1 2 3 4 5 6 7 8 9 10

NOT COMFORTABLE   VERY COMFORTABLE

INVESTING

1 2 3 4 5 6 7 8 9 10

Now go back and rate where you would like to be.

Chapter Two

Generational Welts: Money Beliefs Passed Down Through Silence

Since pretty much the beginning of time, women have often been seen as caretakers, especially due to biological factors, while men have been cast as providers. Men were the hunters, and women the gatherers. This division of roles extended beyond food and family—it infiltrated economics, power, and decision-making. For centuries, money was regarded as a man's domain, while a woman was expected to work within the resources made available to her rather than those she could earn, control, or cultivate for herself. The result isn't just that women lack generational wealth, but they also carry what I call generational welts—deep, inherited scars left by exclusion, silencing, and limitations.

And history backs that up. If we look at the evolution of women's rights over the past 250 years, progress is undeniable, though painfully slow. In 1777, individual states took away women's right to vote. It would be more than 140 years before the Nineteenth Amendment was passed, restoring these voting rights to women. For generations, women could not own property in their own names, open a bank account without a husband or father, or obtain a credit card without a male cosigner. It was not until 1974, just one generation before this was written, that the Equal Credit Opportunity Act made it illegal to deny credit to women on the basis of gender.

This is not ancient history. Many of us were raised by women who lived through these times. Even if they didn't speak about it, we inherited the emotional imprint of that era. This is what many psychologists call emotional inheritance, the passing down of unspoken fears, beliefs, and survival strategies from one generation to the next. For many women, the silence *was* the message.

We don't talk about money.

Don't ask.

Just be careful.

The imprint left by scarcity, survival, or financial trauma doesn't fade simply because circumstances change. Earlier generations had to focus on survival; they lived through real limitations. Today, many women have access to opportunities their mothers or grandmothers never imagined. Yet, they still carry the confusion, caution, or guilt that comes with breaking old patterns. The belief that money is dangerous, ambition is risky, or wanting more is unseemly didn't come from nowhere. It was modeled, reinforced, and passed down, sometimes through words, but often through behaviors.

The treatment of women throughout most of history has left a lasting imprint. This imprint has rippled through generations, influencing the choices we make, the feelings we suppress, and the opportunities we deny ourselves before anyone else has the chance.

To understand just how recent and complex this history is, look at the timeline below. These are just *some* of the key moments that have shaped women's legal and financial agency in the United States over the past 250 years. It's easy to forget

GENERATIONAL WELTS: MONEY BELIEFS PASSED DOWN THROUGH SILENCE

how recent many of these events are, especially when the beliefs passed down to us still carry the weight of the outdated rules.

THE HISTORY OF WOMEN'S RIGHTS

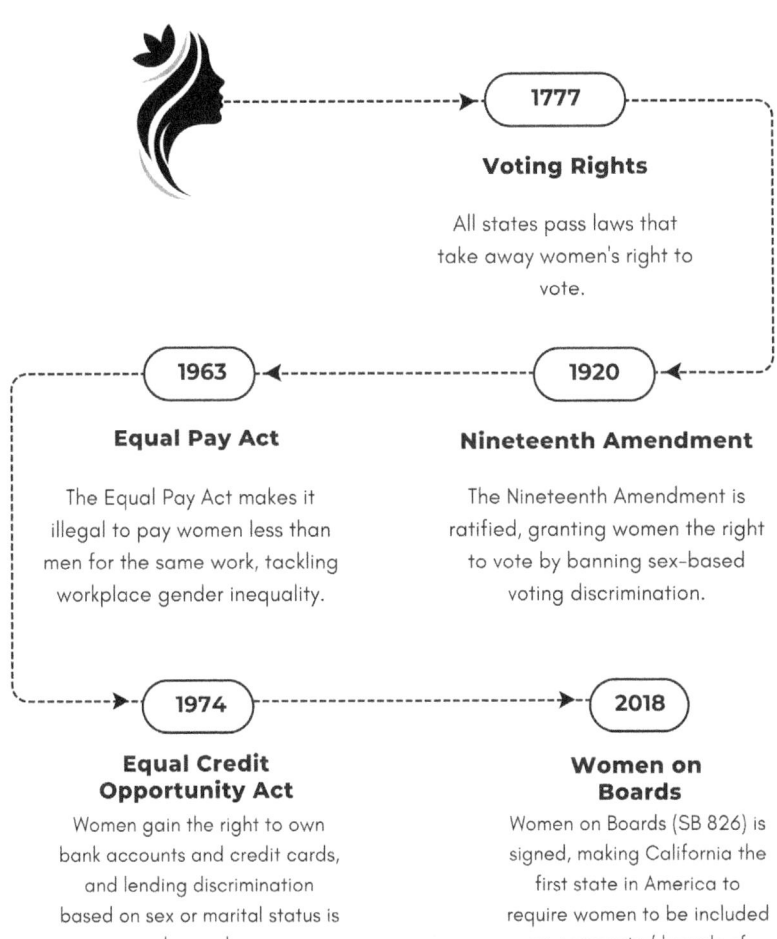

1777 — Voting Rights

All states pass laws that take away women's right to vote.

1920 — Nineteenth Amendment

The Nineteenth Amendment is ratified, granting women the right to vote by banning sex-based voting discrimination.

1963 — Equal Pay Act

The Equal Pay Act makes it illegal to pay women less than men for the same work, tackling workplace gender inequality.

1974 — Equal Credit Opportunity Act

Women gain the right to own bank accounts and credit cards, and lending discrimination based on sex or marital status is banned.

2018 — Women on Boards

Women on Boards (SB 826) is signed, making California the first state in America to require women to be included on companies' boards of directors.

You can download a more detailed graphic of the History of Women's Rights on my website at www.marciadawood.com/wealth

You don't have to look far to see the impact of this inheritance. I've heard countless stories from women who are smart, capable, and financially stable—yet still feel unsure, unworthy, or uncomfortable when it comes to money. This doesn't manifest in one big, dramatic moment; rather, it appears in patterns. Like the woman who stayed in a job she had outgrown for five years too long because it felt "secure," even though she quietly resented being underpaid and undervalued. Or the mother who insisted on managing every family expense on her own, even when it strained her, because her own mother had taught her that financial dependence was dangerous. This mindset appears in the entrepreneur who can't seem to raise her prices without offering a discount, even when clients don't ask for one. It also shows in the friend who earns a good salary but still double- and triple-checks every nonessential purchase—not because she can't afford it, but because spending on herself still feels uncomfortable.

These aren't isolated stories; they form part of a shared emotional legacy. Quiet patterns of shrinking, sacrificing, and second-guessing passed from one generation to the next. While the names and details change, the root cause remains the same: a deeply embedded belief that money isn't fully theirs to claim or control. That asking for more, spending with confidence, or building real wealth carries emotional risk, even when it no longer comes with legal or literal barriers.

Take a moment here.

Where and how have these beliefs shown up in your own life?

Have you ever hesitated to ask for more, even when you knew you were qualified?

Have you ever downplayed your success to make others feel more comfortable?

Have you ever felt guilty spending on yourself, even when you could afford it?

Generational Welts: Money Beliefs Passed Down Through Silence

These moments may seem small, but they carry profound meaning. They are signs of something deeper: beliefs that were never truly yours to begin with, yet silently influencing your choices and limiting your wealth and power.

The Cost of Silence

So many women remain silent in rooms where they could ask questions, set boundaries, or negotiate better terms. Not because they lack something to say, but because they have been conditioned to believe that speaking up is risky. That asking for clarity makes them look unqualified. That wanting more seems greedy. That taking up space could backfire.

I remember the first angel investing meeting I attended back in 2012. I was one of the few women in the room. It was intimidating. Everyone else seemed to know the lingo, the process, the right questions to ask. I felt like an outsider. Like I didn't belong, and that any question I asked might expose that. So, I kept quiet. I stayed small. Fortunately, I was among people who were very welcoming and encouraged me to ask questions over the next several months as I learned. They helped me get over that feeling of being an outsider.

More recently, I have seen women step into all kinds of spaces boldly—not only showing up but also creating environments where others, too, feel welcome. Places where we can ask the so-called dumb questions without shame. Where curiosity is encouraged and confidence is built, not assumed. I love seeing these opportunities being presented, and I love watching women seize them even more. And the beauty is our strength grows when we stand together, not in competition. We are at our strongest when we fix each other's crowns, not when we try to knock them off. Every time a woman claims her voice, pulls up another chair, or opens a new door, she nudges the needle forward while reshaping the future for all of us. And that gives me great hope for the next generations, who will inherit a world where boldness, belonging, and abundance are the norm.

Because it matters how we react in these moments, whether in a boardroom, on a video call, or during a conversation with a friend. Our reactions either reinforce our beliefs or challenge them.

I still remember a conversation that stuck with me. I was with a group of friends, casually talking about what we were working on at the time. I said, "I'm writing a short speech, like a TED Talk."

Without missing a beat, one of the guys turned to me and said, "You know, they don't let just anyone give a TED Talk."

It hit me like a punch I didn't see coming. I laughed it off, trying not to show how much it landed. "Well, it's a TED-style talk I'm writing," I said, shrinking the moment. Shrinking *myself*.

I still think about that exchange. Not just because of what he said—but because of what I didn't say.

I wish I'd looked him straight in the eye and asked, "Why couldn't that be me?"

Instead, I let him take the air out of the room. I let his doubt become my own, even if only for a moment.

That moment stayed with me. Not as a failure, but as fuel. It taught me how quietly we internalize other people's skepticism. It reminded me how easy it is to shrink and how important it is to push back, kindly but clearly.

And then on October 29, 2022, I stepped onto the stage with the big red dot at TEDxCharlotte and gave that talk.

You Are Enough

Ironically, the morning after I wrote the previous section about staying quiet in rooms, a friend of mine, Charlene Wheeless, author of *You Are Enough!*, posted something on Instagram that stopped me in my tracks. She opened with these words:

"I spent years shrinking myself to fit into rooms that needed my full power."

Generational Welts: Money Beliefs Passed Down Through Silence

She went on to talk about playing small, about hiding parts of herself, about waiting—sometimes consciously, sometimes not—for someone to give her permission to show up fully. Until one day, she realized: "No one was going to give me permission to show up as myself. That was my job."

And from that moment, Charlene claimed her space. Boldly. Unapologetically.

Charlene's story is remarkable. As a young Black girl, she was told when she tried out for the cheerleading team that she'd be the fourth alternate—a message meant to shrink her expectations. But she didn't let that stop her. She went on to become an NFL cheerleader. And even after that success, when she moved into the corporate world and built an incredibly successful career, she wrestled with the feeling that she didn't quite fit in.

Her journey is a powerful reminder that no level of achievement automatically erases the old beliefs we carry. You can accomplish extraordinary things and still feel the urge to shrink. You can fill the résumé, win the awards, earn the title—and still must choose to take up your space.

Charlene's experience also highlights how inherited patterns compound for women navigating multiple identities. As a Black woman, she didn't just inherit messages about women staying small—she also carried the weight of stereotypes about who belongs in certain spaces, who can be confident without being labeled aggressive, and whose success is questioned or minimized. The intersection of gender and race created additional layers of caution, more reasons to shrink, and more voices saying, "Don't take up too much space."

Yet Charlene also inherited something powerful: a legacy of resilience, determination, and the courage to create opportunities where none existed. The same family lines that passed down caution also passed down strength, resourcefulness, and an unshakeable belief in the power of persistence. When she stepped onto that NFL field, she wasn't just claiming her own space—she was honoring generations of women who had fought for the right to be seen, to be valued, and to be celebrated in spaces not designed for them.

Charlene's post felt perfectly aligned, just like her story, which reminds us that we don't need to wait for anyone else's permission to share.

See Charlene's full post in the box below.

---

charwheeless I spent years shrinking myself to fit into rooms that needed my full power.

It took me years to admit that... even to myself.

Early in my career, I believed that if I kept my head down, worked twice as hard, and never ruffled feathers, I'd make it.

I thought success meant being seen but never heard too much.

Accepted, but not truly known.

But deep down, I was playing small.

Hiding...

My story.
My ideas.
My real voice.

Afraid that if I stood out, I'd be pushed out.

One day, after another meeting where I'd held back yet another idea, I looked in the mirror and barely recognized the woman staring back at me.

That was my wake-up call.

I realized:

No one was going to give me permission to show up as myself. That was my job.

So I stopped waiting for a seat at the table and started claiming my space.

Fully.
Boldly.
Unapologetically.

And you know what happened?
Everything changed.

People listened.
Doors opened.

I felt more alive, more authentic, and more impactful than ever before.

If you feel yourself shrinking in any room → stop.

The world needs you at your full power.

Your story, your voice, your leadership—it all matters.

Don't wait for permission to be who you already are.

You are enough → exactly as you are.

#YouAreEnough #AuthenticLeadership #Unapologetic
#WomenInLeadership #CharleneWheeless

Generational Welts: Money Beliefs Passed Down Through Silence

Charlene's story may seem extraordinary, but the truth is this choice is available to all of us. You don't need to be on a big stage or in a high-powered role to ask yourself, *Am I still waiting for permission? Am I still holding back, shrinking, or hiding parts of myself to fit into spaces that actually need my full power?* You don't need to have all the answers right now. Just start noticing. Awareness is where change begins.

Inherited Through DNA?

Can mindset really be passed down from generation to generation without us even realizing it?

Until now, this chapter has focused on passing down messages through actions or behaviors, but what if there is even more to it? While reading *Deeper Than Money* by Chloe Elise, I was reminded of a study conducted by researchers at Emory University. In the experiment, mice were exposed to the scent of cherry blossoms while receiving mild electric shocks to their feet. Over time, the mice began to associate the scent of cherry blossoms with pain and fear. Eventually, the shock was no longer necessary; the scent alone triggered anxiety.

But here's where it gets interesting: the offspring of those mice, who were never shocked themselves, *also* showed signs of fear when exposed to the cherry blossom scent. They had inherited a fear response to something they had never personally experienced.

And it didn't stop there. The *grandchildren* of the original mice, two generations removed from the initial trauma, still responded with fear. No shocks. No training. Just inherited anxiety triggered by the scent. Whoa.

Imagine how this translates to humans. Not only have many women watched their mothers and grandmothers struggle with money, juggling bills, putting others first, or staying silent about financial decisions, but the idea of holding back has been deeply encoded. Through both lived experience and, yes, epigenetics (how trauma and environment can influence what gets passed down through generations), we inherit more than just memories; we inherit reactions, beliefs, and patterns. The message that money is not something to be bold with but something to manage quietly and cautiously often allows guilt to creep in. You don't have to be explicitly taught for that message to reside within you. Sometimes, it is simply and silently passed down through behavior, generation to generation.

Take Rachel, for example. She is a leadership coach for midsize businesses, with over a decade of experience helping teams grow, navigate change, and lead effectively. She spent years working at a respected consulting firm, earning praise from clients and colleagues alike. Now, she has finally taken the leap to start her own business.

On paper, she's more than ready. But when it comes time to set her rates, she falters. She researches what others are charging, especially her male counterparts with similar or even less experience, and sees that her initial rates are significantly lower. Still, she hesitates to raise them.

She tells herself, *This is strategic.* That she is just getting started. That clients won't pay those higher rates unless she has been on her own longer. But beneath these surface justifications lies something deeper—a quiet, persistent belief that asking for more might push people away. That she must "earn her place" all over again. That charging what she's truly worth might come off as too aggressive.

She was never taught to undervalue herself. No one directly told her that she couldn't charge what she's worth. But like the mice in the cherry blossom study, she responds to a signal she has internalized—one rooted in years of observing women being praised for humility, practicality, and self-sacrifice rather than boldness or self-advocacy.

She's not charging less because she lacks experience.

She's charging less because part of her still questions whether she has the right to take up that much space.

And she's far from alone.

Of course, the specific messages women inherit about money vary dramatically depending on their family structure, cultural background, and socioeconomic history. For some women, the inherited pattern isn't just about staying small; it's about survival in a much more literal sense.

A first-generation immigrant might carry her mother's fear that any financial misstep could threaten her family's stability in a new country. The message isn't "don't ask for too much," but rather "hold on to what you have at all costs." A woman whose grandmother cleaned houses to support her family during the Depression might inherit a different kind of caution: the belief that financial security comes only through multiple income streams and constant vigilance, making it difficult to invest in herself or take calculated risks.

Women from working-class backgrounds often inherit a contradictory message: take pride in self-reliance, yet treat wealth with suspicion. They might excel at stretching a dollar but struggle with the idea that they deserve to earn significantly more than their parents ever did. Meanwhile, women from affluent families might carry their own burden: the pressure to maintain appearances, the guilt around inherited privilege, or the sense of inferiority that their success isn't truly earned.

These different starting points matter because they shape not only how women think about money but also which financial strategies feel accessible or appropriate. Networking events that help some women build wealth might feel exclusionary to others. Investment approaches that make sense for the generationally wealthy might seem irrelevant to someone building their family's financial foundation.

We Stand at a Cultural Crossroads

We may not have created the beliefs we hold about money, but we are the ones carrying them now, and with that comes a responsibility. The fear, the guilt, and the pressure to stay small were survival tools for generations of women who came before us. They did what they had to do in a world that offered them few choices. But times have changed. Yet the old mindset persists—not because it still fits, but because it was passed down without question. That said, not all of us grew up with silence or scarcity. Some women were raised by strong role models—mothers, grandmothers, or mentors—who handled money with clarity, strength, and intention. Those examples matter too, because they show us what's possible when power and purpose are linked.

But those were exceptions rather than the rule. We need to break these old mindset patterns. If we don't, we not only keep ourselves stuck, but we also pass that burden on to the next generation. Our daughters, nieces, and other young women learn how to relate to money based on how we handle it. If we model fear, silence, and self-sacrifice, they will adopt these behaviors. If we diminish our ambition or apologize for our success, they will follow our example.

This isn't just about individual personal growth. It's about generational change and it will take more than one generation. We are the in-between generations, regardless of age. We are the ones with the unique opportunity to rewrite the script: to normalize abundance, demonstrate holding power with grace, build wealth without guilt, and make values-aligned choices without apology.

We can't change the past, but we can choose what the future will inherit.

And choosing differently begins with something quieter—recognition.

The women who begin to break old money patterns don't do so by flipping their entire lives overnight. Instead, they do it through small, intentional choices that build progressively. They recognize the moment they are vulnerable to diminishing their success, and they pause. They catch themselves underpricing a proposal, and they raise the number. They hear that old voice

GENERATIONAL WELTS: MONEY BELIEFS PASSED DOWN THROUGH SILENCE

whispering "don't ask" and they inquire anyway—for the raise, for the support, for the clarity they need.

This graphic is a depiction of where we are now as a society and where we will ideally move to, to empower future generations.

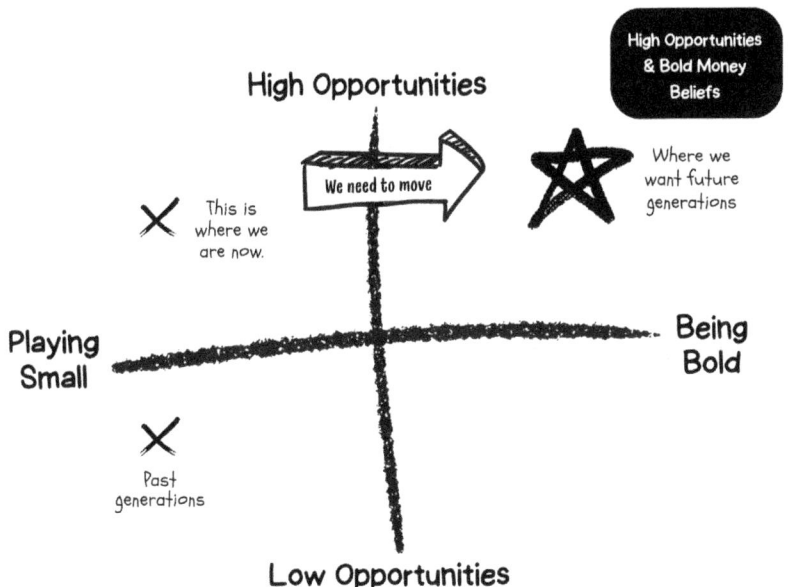

As mentioned in Charlene's story, the shift begins with awareness, learning to spot the difference between your own instincts and inherited beliefs passed down like a family heirloom. That knot in your stomach before a salary conversation might be the echo of a past generation trying to stay safe. You can honor that voice for what it meant then while still choosing a response that serves who you are now.

This isn't about discarding everything you've been taught. Some of those lessons— being prepared, thinking things through, assessing risks—are valuable. The key is learning to tell the difference between wisdom and worry. Between strategic caution and fear.

In the chapters ahead, we'll explore how to identify inherited patterns, retain what is useful, and develop a money mindset that reflects both who you are and who you are becoming.

The goal isn't perfection.

It's presence.

It's intention.

And it begins with remembering that you have more power to shift these patterns than you might realize.

Exercise: Your Money Timeline

Every money choice you make today is influenced by the experiences, stories, and lessons you've picked up throughout your life, often without even realizing it.

Some beliefs come from your family, others from your culture, and still others from personal victories or setbacks. Together, they form the invisible script that shapes how you think and feel about money.

The Your Money Timeline exercise gives you a new perspective by putting everything in one place. By identifying the key money moments in your life, you'll begin to recognize the patterns, beliefs, and pivotal moments that have shaped your current relationship with money.

This will give you the perspective to understand the evolution of your money story, so you can decide which parts to keep and which parts to rewrite.

When you see your money story laid out in front of you, you'll begin to connect the dots in unexpected ways. Try not to filter or judge. We will revisit this timeline later in the book as you start to reshape your unapologetic future.

I know that not everyone is an exercise person. Some people love them; some people don't. That's okay. These aren't workouts or homework. They are simply tools you can try out along the way. Take what helps, leave what doesn't, and let them support you in your own way.

GENERATIONAL WELTS: MONEY BELIEFS PASSED DOWN THROUGH SILENCE

Use the space provided, or take a blank sheet of paper, and draw a horizontal line representing your life from early childhood to the present day.

Now, think back and begin marking key money moments along that timeline. These could include:

- Times when money felt scarce or abundant
- Moments when you got in trouble for either spending or saving money
- Family conflicts or major decisions involving money
- Unspoken rules you have absorbed about "what money means"
- Lessons you have learned from school, media, culture, or religion
- Any time money made you feel powerful, ashamed, confused, or proud

Also, consider how your parents and grandparents managed money, as this may influence the key events on your timeline. You may choose to write positive memories above the line and less positive memories below it.

Write down short notes, codes, or symbols at each point. You don't need to capture everything—just what stands out.

Once your timeline is complete, take a step back and reflect:

- What patterns or themes do you notice?
- Which messages about money have stayed with you?
- Which of those beliefs or habits still serve you?
- Which ones are you ready to question or let go of?

This exercise isn't about judging the past; it's about understanding the emotional and cultural blueprint you have inherited so that you can choose what comes next.

Now, take the answers and reflections you have uncovered and reshape them into positive, empowering statements. For instance, if your timeline shows, "I was always told money was tight, so I felt guilty asking for things," you could reframe it as, "I value being resourceful, and I'm learning that it's okay to invest in myself and my future."

This exercise, like the others in this book, is especially effective when shared—whether with a friend, partner, family member, or group. Discussing money with others can lead to meaningful conversations that strengthen bonds and promote mutual understanding. You might discover shared experiences, different perspectives, or inherited beliefs that you were previously unaware of or that greatly differ from your own. Money is often seen as a private or even taboo topic, but when discussed openly with honesty and care, it loses much of its stigma and gains real power.

Exercise: A Letter to Money: Rewriting the Relationship

Our relationship with money is rarely formed intentionally; instead, it is often shaped over time by both explicit and implicit messages and lessons.

This exercise offers you a chance to pause and articulate what has remained unspoken. Writing a letter to money may seem unusual at first, but it's a powerful way to gain clarity about how you truly feel. It helps you identify what you've internalized, where you've held back, and where you might be ready to move forward.

There's no need to filter or edit, and you don't have to preserve the letter if you don't want to. This letter is just for you. It

Generational Welts: Money Beliefs Passed Down Through Silence

can be raw, tender, or messy. You may want to express frustration, gratitude, regret, hope, or all of the above.

The goal isn't to find the perfect words; it's to listen to your own voice and give yourself permission to feel, identify, and begin reshaping your money story.

When you see your feelings written down, they lose some of their grip. In that space, something new can begin.

Here are a few examples of how other letters concerning money began:

Example 1:

Dear Money,

For a long time, I have blamed you for my stress, my shame, and my scarcity. I thought if I just had more of you, everything would feel better. But the truth is ... I have never truly learned how to feel safe with you. You felt like a test I was always failing.

I want that to change. I want to understand you, not fear you. I'm tired of pretending I don't care when I really do. I'm ready to stop running and start building something real between us.

Example 2:

Dear Money,

We've had a complicated relationship. I've chased you, avoided you, and sometimes even resented you. But now I want to start over.

I'm ready to take responsibility for how I treat you. I want to stop passing you off to others. I want to understand how you function, how you grow, and how we can move forward together.

I'm not asking you to fix everything; I'm asking for a clean slate.

Now it's your turn. Take a few minutes to write your own letter to money. Here are a few sample lines to help you get started:

- "Dear Money, I was taught that you meant…"
- "I've spent too long feeling ___ about you…"
- "From this point forward, I want our relationship to feel like…"

There's no right way to do this. Just write what's true for you. This is your moment to express what has been left unsaid and to make space for something new.

_____
_____
_____
_____
_____
_____
_____
_____
_____
_____
_____
_____
_____
_____
_____
_____
_____
_____

Chapter Three

The Quiet Grip of Money Guilt

So far, we have discussed money guilt and playing small. Before we move on, it's important to clarify that these are not the same, although they can sometimes be linked.

Money guilt is an internal feeling. It's the emotion you carry: shame, fear, discomfort, or anxiety related to wanting, having, or using money. It's the voice in your head that whispers, *Who am I to want this?* or *This is too much.*

Playing small is an external behavior. It refers to the actions (or inactions) you take when you hold yourself back, shrink, or play it safe, even when no one is explicitly telling you to do so.

In other words, guilt is something you feel, while playing small is something you do.

Without awareness of your feelings, change isn't possible in your actions. We'll explore where money guilt manifests, how it influences your decisions and behaviors, and how you can begin to loosen its grip. Once you recognize the emotional patterns you carry, you can start reclaiming your power—not just over your bank account but also over your thoughts, feelings, and actions related to money and beyond.

When Success Feels Heavy

Selfish.

Marissa could hear the voice in her head as she eyed the handbag in the boutique window. Soft caramel leather. A gold clasp that caught the light just enough. It was elegant, understated, and... expensive. Too expensive, according to the voice.

She had never spent that much money on a handbag—not even close. Her bags were always practical, neutral, and almost always on sale. However, this one felt different. It was beautiful, yes, but it also felt indulgent. Unjustifiable.

You don't need that. Who do you think you are?

That money could be spent on something better—something more useful.

A gift for someone else. A donation. Savings.

It sat in the boutique window just a block from her office, all that soft caramel leather and gold hardware. Not flashy, but confident. It looked like something that belonged to a woman who knew exactly what she was doing. Marissa stared at it the way someone might gaze at a version of themselves they didn't believe they were allowed to become.

Still, she couldn't shake the guilt. Every time she thought about walking into the store and trying it on her shoulder, something tightened in her chest. *That money could be spent on something better.* The guilt wasn't just about the cost—it was about the message: she believed she wasn't worth spending that much money on.

Then she heard about the weight loss pool.

Her sister's wedding was three months away, and a few friends had started a challenge. Each would contribute $100, and the person who reached their goal weight first would take the pot. Marissa joined without hesitation. Not only did she want to lose weight before the wedding, but she also thought about the prize money, which would cover the cost of that bag if she won. That made a difference.

She printed a photo of the bag and displayed it on her desk. It became her daily reminder. Not just of the wedding, or the weight, but of wanting something for herself and allowing herself to pursue it.

She found a drive she hadn't felt in years. She planned her meals, took walks after dinner, and cut the mindless snacking. And every time she doubted herself, she looked at that photo.

The week eight weigh-in had arrived. She felt so nervous as she stepped onto the scale, but sure enough, she was half a pound under her goal weight. She had done it. She had won. And, of course, the first thing she did was march straight into the boutique to buy the bag. It was the first time in years she had given herself something with no strings attached. No discount code, no justification, no "I'll just wait and see." Just yes.

The moment she held it in her hands, it felt like a victory. Not just for the weight loss but for the commitment, the follow-through, and the decision to choose herself.

But then came the wedding.

The bag no longer felt like a triumph. Instead, it felt loud and out of place. Suddenly self-conscious, she wondered if she was showing off or if it was simply too much.

Her sister beamed all night, gracious and glowing, while Marissa kept thinking about the blender she had bought from the registry. Should she have spent the prize money on a better gift? Was the handbag too selfish?

She had worked so hard. She won that money. Didn't she deserve to spend it on herself?

But deserving and feeling deserving turned out to be two very different things.

She repeatedly reminded herself; *I earned this.* Yet the feeling didn't take hold. Guilt continued to surface.

And the weight? It didn't stay off. Within a few months, it crept back on, accompanied by quiet shame. The bag, once a trophy, began to feel like a reminder of the weight she had lost and regained, of the money she had dared to spend on herself, and of the confidence that had bloomed only to fade away.

She stopped using it. It sat at the back of her closet, tucked inside its dust bag like a secret.

Marissa's story is about more than spending guilt; it's about the weight of worth. It explores the complex burden women carry regarding desire, success, and permission. However, the guilt surrounding money doesn't only manifest when we spend it. It also appears in other ways: having money, lacking it, desiring it, and wanting it too much. And the list goes on.

Which brings us to Elena.

Elena never thought money would make her feel uncomfortable.

She was thirty-six and a product manager at a well-known company—one of those names people recognize. One that has been a public company for years and was known for offering good compensation, particularly in stock options. Although her salary was impressive, it was the equity that transformed her financial situation. Every quarter brought a new vesting date, another block of shares, and another moment for her to gaze at her account balance and wonder how everything had progressed so quickly.

Her husband, George, had taken a job at a midsize logistics firm while they were still figuring things out. It wasn't flashy, but he believed in what they were building. He stayed with the company for nearly a decade, enduring slow quarters and leadership changes, until it was finally acquired by a larger company. The acquisition wasn't front-page news, but it brought in a substantial amount of money.

And then, just a few months later, they welcomed their first baby.

The Quiet Grip of Money Guilt

That's when things got complicated—not at home, surprisingly. Sure, they were sleep-deprived and constantly scrolling for advice on how to care for this new being in their lives, but they were managing okay. The awkward part came outside the house, in the mom groups that Elena joined right after her son was born.

She wanted what everyone desires in those early months: someone else who understands. Someone who knows what it feels like to live on three hours of sleep and find nourishment in one-handed snacks.

But the conversations kept circling back to money.

"How are diapers this expensive?"

"I didn't realize day care would cost more than our mortgage."

"I'm going to have to go back to work earlier than I had planned. We simply can't afford the time off."

Elena would nod along, saying things like, "Yeah, it adds up fast," or "It's so tough," and then quickly change the subject. What was she supposed to say?

She wasn't worried about money. She wasn't cutting back or stressing about daycare. They had already set aside money for preschool and were more than comfortable financially. Yet, she felt guilty. Not for having the money, but for the awkwardness she felt when discussing it without sounding out of touch.

She hated the feeling. Like she was hiding a secret. Like she didn't belong.

They weren't flashy. Their house was nice but modest. She still drove her six-year-old car. Her clothes were from the same places she shopped before they were doing so well. But when conversations turned to financial stress, she didn't know what to say.

At night, when the baby finally went to sleep and the house was quiet, Elena would sit on the couch with her laptop open, trying to make sense of it all. The numbers didn't lie. They were doing well. Extremely well. But she didn't feel rich. She felt isolated.

She wondered what story she'd tell her son one day. How his parents came into money, not all at once, but gradually. How privilege can sneak up on you, and how it changes the conversations you can have.

And sometimes, even when you've done everything right, you find yourself in rooms where you can't quite tell the truth.

There is so much to unpack here.

On the surface, money guilt might look like feeling bad for buying something frivolous. However beneath that, it is more complex and far more common than we often admit. Marissa felt guilty for spending, while Elena felt guilty for having. Two very different financial realities. The same emotional tension.

Because money guilt isn't one-size-fits-all. It shows up in many forms: guilt for spending, for saving too much, for not saving enough. Guilt for having money. Guilt for not having it. Guilt for wanting more. Guilt for wanting anything at all. Sometimes, we feel guilty for struggling, and other times, we feel guilty for not struggling.

Additionally, we are taught from an early age that talking about money is rude, inappropriate, or off-putting to others. As a result, instead of being honest, we put on a performance. We nod in agreement. We minimize our possessions or hide what we have. We share half-truths or completely change the subject. Like Elena, we find ourselves in rooms where we feel unable to tell the truth, not because anyone taught us so, but because we have internalized the belief that silence is safer.

But staying quiet comes at a cost.

It isolates us. It causes us to compare our lives to carefully curated versions of others, which is so easy with today's technology, like Gina seeing pictures on Gwen's social media. It prevents us from seeking advice, support, or even celebration. It also leads us to deceptively believe that we are the only ones feeling this way.

What we spend money on is deeply personal. For Marissa, it was a handbag. For someone else, it might be a car, a vacation, or a luxury mattress. Some people spend thousands on ski gear

The Quiet Grip of Money Guilt

and season passes each year and love every minute of it. Personally, I have no interest in racing downhill with large objects strapped to my feet, but that's just me. I would prefer to spend my time and money on a yoga retreat or a hiking trip to a place like Sedona. The point is that everyone has a different priority pulse when it comes to money. What feels wasteful to one person might seem meaningful to another. Both perspectives are valid.

Maybe we look at someone else's spending and feel confused, critical, or even judgmental. But these reactions often reveal more about ourselves than about them. What we notice in other people's choices frequently reflects our own values, fears, beliefs, or hang-ups about money. When we catch ourselves reacting this way, we can pause and ask, *Am I being judgy?* Take a moment to get curious about what's underneath our own response.

We all value things differently. The problem isn't what we value; it's the way we're taught to judge ourselves and others on those values. And the way guilt slips in and takes over, often without us even noticing.

That's why I'm writing this book.

The problem is caused by years of conditioning, silence, guilt, and outdated beliefs that tell women to be modest, selfless, cautious, and reserved when discussing money.

It's not that women aren't good with money.

It's the guilt and all the stories we've been told about what we should do with money that keep getting in the way.

For some women, guilt arises over money they didn't directly earn, whether it came through an inheritance, a divorce settlement, or even winning the lottery. Instead of feeling entitled to use and enjoy it, they often feel awkward, apologetic, or compelled to justify every dollar—as if money only counts when earned through a paycheck. This mindset runs deep and causes many women to second-guess or minimize resources they already have. But no matter how your money arrives—whether through hard work, inheritance, luck, or life circumstances—it's still yours to claim. Claim it unapologetically.

Whether you are spending it, saving it, earning it, or wanting more of it, you have the right to take up space in your financial life. You are allowed to make money decisions that reflect your values, not your guilt.

And most importantly, you are allowed to talk about it. The more we do, the less power the shame holds.

Spending and Value

Money guilt can take many forms, and it doesn't always announce itself loudly. Often, it appears quietly in the background of daily choices, slipping unnoticed into your thoughts and actions.

For example, you might feel guilty when you spend money on yourself, even if you can comfortably afford it. Perhaps you hesitate when it comes to something meaningful—a vacation that recharges you, an experience that excites you, a piece of clothing that uplifts you—because a voice inside says, *That's indulgent; you don't really need that.* You end up denying it to yourself, not because spending on yourself is financially unwise, but because it feels selfish.

But guilt doesn't appear only when we face major decisions. Sometimes it's there even in small, forgettable choices—the ones we barely notice but make every single day.

Like the time I moved into a new place and needed to buy a paper towel holder for the kitchen. Nothing fancy, just something to sit on the counter. I went to the store and found two options. One was basic. It simply held the roll. The other had a small arm that secured the paper towel roll in place, allowing you to tear off a sheet with one hand. Game-changing convenience. The difference? Five bucks.

And yet, I actually debated it. I stood there in the aisle thinking, *Do I really need this fancier version? It's just a paper towel holder. What's the big deal?* As if spending an extra five dollars were such an indulgence, I would be living a whole new life of countertop luxury.

But I use that paper towel holder every day. Think about how many sheets are on each roll and how many rolls I use in a year. I ended up buying the extravagant paper towel holder, and now I get the satisfaction of that little arm doing its job every single time I use it. It's efficient. It's helpful. And it's proof that sometimes choosing the better option—the one that actually supports your everyday life—is not indulgent. It's simply practical.

Looking back, it's wild how much brain space I gave to that five-dollar decision. And yet, we do this all the time. We shrink. We minimize. We choose the "lesser than" option, not because we have to, but because somewhere deep down, we think it is the right thing to do, even when the decision is something we may live with, use, wear, or look at for quite some time.

That's the odd thing about value. We all interpret it differently. Sometimes usefulness matters, while other times perception matters. We like to see ourselves as rational, but what something is worth can be influenced by context, branding, and even presentation.

Payless, the discount shoe retailer, made this clear in 2018 when they launched a fake luxury brand called Palessi. Payless created a stylish pop-up boutique in Los Angeles, stocked it with their usual $15 to $40 shoes, and invited influencers to explore the display. Everything was arranged to feel upscale—gold decor, glass shelves, and dramatic lighting. The twist? They increased the prices by hundreds of dollars. Some pairs sold for over $600.[vi]

The shoes didn't change. But people's perception of them did. Influencers praised the design, describing the shoes as elegant and high-quality. Many bought them, fully convinced they were investing in luxury. When the stunt was revealed, it wasn't just a punchline—it was a mirror. The same product, presented in a different context, created an entirely different reaction.

A similar dynamic played out in an experiment featured on the TV show *Brain Games*. At a booth, people were offered two identical cakes—same recipe, same ingredients, same baker. One was labeled fifteen dollars, the other fifty-five. The cheaper cake was described as drier and less flavorful. The more expensive one? Richer, moister, more "worth it." Again, nothing about the cakes themselves was different—only the price.[vii]

We often get caught up in false narratives about what's worth spending money on and what isn't. This is why money guilt can be so tricky. Sometimes, we second-guess purchasing a five dollar paper towel holder that makes our life better every day, but some wouldn't hesitate to spend a hundred dollars on a dinner if the restaurant has dim lighting and pretty linens. We don't just buy things; we buy stories, and we tend to undervalue the ones that aren't linked in some way to prestige.

Sometimes, the things with the highest value don't come with a high price tag, and the things with the highest price tag don't always provide real value. We have been taught to see price as a shortcut for quality, status, or importance, but that shortcut often misleads us. Value isn't about how much something costs; it's about what it adds to your life. How it aligns with your needs, your context, your priorities. A low-cost item can be very valuable, while a high-cost one can be all surface. The key is learning to tell those signals apart and trust your own sense of what matters, not just the numbers on a tag.

Just Because It's Free Doesn't Mean You Should Eat It

Money guilt shows up in many forms and can weave itself into our everyday thinking, including the idea of getting our money's worth. We have been conditioned to believe that value means squeezing every last drop from what we have paid for, even when it no longer serves us. Redefining value means permitting ourselves to choose ease, joy, and alignment instead of focusing on frugality alone. For women, this shift is powerful because it transforms money from a source of stress into a source of support. But what does it look like when value is out of alignment?

The Quiet Grip of Money Guilt

Melissa wasn't sure what to wear to the holiday party. She didn't want to buy a new outfit since she had already paid for the party ticket. So, she squeezed into something sparkly from her closet, found shoes she knew wouldn't hurt her feet too much, and showed up ready to make it count.

And she did.

Champagne upon arrival. White wine by the sushi station. Something intriguing in a fancy glass named The Ornament Express. She lost track somewhere around drink number five. By the end of the night, she was dancing with strangers and professing her undying love for hummus.

Two days later, still nursing a headache and sending her friends texts like, "My liver has filed for divorce," she concluded with a proud declaration:

Well . . . at least I got my money's worth.

For Melissa, the prolonged hangover didn't have to be the outcome. She got stuck in a mindset—the belief that value means squeezing every last drop from something, even when it ultimately left her filled with regret.

It's the same reason why we eat the complimentary bread at restaurants, even when we're not hungry.

Why we grab every snack or drink at an event just because it's included.

Why we collect hotel's mini soap, mini shampoo, and mini sewing kit—despite never having used any of them, ever.

There's something wired into us that says, *If I've paid for it (or someone has), I should take it or eat it or use it.*

We confuse access with obligation. We don't need to eat it just because it's free; we don't need to take it just because it's included, and we don't need to collect it just because it feels like we aren't wasting it. What we do need is to take a step back, reflect on what we truly want in our lives, and work toward achieving that.

The Subscription Mentality

Subscriptions have quietly taken over our lives and budgets. Not to mention, they add a whole new level of mental gymnastics to our thoughts on money. Increasingly, how we live involves a monthly fee: for gyms, streaming platforms, productivity apps, and meal kits. You pay a flat rate, and then the race begins to get your money's worth.

Let's dig into online streaming services. You don't pay per show. You pay once, then it is all-you-can-watch. So the more you binge, the more justified the price feels. The worth of each individual show isn't the primary focus—it's about volume.

It rewires how we think. Instead of asking, "Do I want this?" we ask, "Am I using this enough to justify the cost?"

That question sounds smart. But it can lead us into a trap.

We start tallying usage instead of measuring impact.

We watch shows we are not enjoying.

We go to classes we do not like.

We keep subscriptions alive just because we might use them next month.

All to avoid feeling like we wasted money. But here's the irony: the real waste occurs when we continue to invest our time, energy, and attention into things that no longer serve us—just so we can feel like we used them *enough*.

These feelings are not just prevalent in subscriptions. My example involves an expensive face cream I bought. Deep down, I didn't really like it. I kept telling myself I just needed to give it some time. It felt sticky. But at this point, I knew I couldn't return it, so I quietly stopped using it and put it in a drawer. Then, when I tried another product, the same thing happened. Even when I found one I liked by the third try, I was still hesitant to throw the others away.

We hold onto things we're not using because we don't want to admit they were a mistake. The money's already gone, but the guilt lingers. So, the stuff piles up.

The Quiet Grip of Money Guilt

Letting go creates space. Not just in your drawer, but in how you make choices going forward. You learn to stop justifying what doesn't work and start trusting what does.

Back to Melissa and the holiday party. The drinks were flowing. The vibes were high. But when the lights came back on and the glitter had settled, the real question wasn't, "Did she get her money's worth?"

"Was it worth it, for her?"

Not in quantity. Not in cocktails. But in experience, in memory, in alignment.

Real value isn't about how much you can squeeze out. It's about what fits. What feels right. What adds meaning or ease or joy to your life, without demanding more than it provides.

You don't need to keep eating at the buffet even after you're full.

You don't need to binge-watch a show to justify your subscription.

And you definitely don't need to pocket the hotel soap like it's a badge of conservation.

Sometimes restraint is the better choice.

Sometimes having less makes it more valuable.

True value is personal. It's not about metrics or usage stats. It's not about getting your money's worth like a receipt would reflect. Instead, it's about how something fits into your life, meets your needs, and contributes to your peace of mind.

Melissa could've had one drink, one laugh, one new connection—and that might have been more than enough.

Next time you are tempted to squeeze every last drop from something just because you can, ask yourself instead:

"Does this actually matter to me?"

That's where real value begins.

Having, Wanting, and Winning

Spending guilt is one thing. But guilt isn't always tied to a purchase. Sometimes, it appears in what you already own, the life you've built, the milestones you've reached, and the money you've earned. Perhaps you've achieved a career goal, grown your business, or negotiated a well-deserved raise, but instead of celebrating, you hold back. You downplay your success around friends or family, subtly adjusting how you talk about your work or income. You tell yourself it's about being humble or relatable, but beneath the surface, there's something else: a fear that your success might create distance, discomfort, or resentment.

Take Dana, for example. Dana is the Chief Financial Officer (CFO) at a midsize company. She has worked hard to get there, with years of experience, long nights, and tough decisions. And yet, when she is at a party or chatting with new people, she never says she is a CFO. She says, "Oh, I work in finance," and quickly changes the subject.

Why?

Because she doesn't want people to think she's showing off.

Because she doesn't want to make anyone feel uncomfortable.

Because part of her believes that having more visibility, more authority, or more financial power makes her "too much."

This kind of guilt runs deep. It tells us that if we succeed, we will be judged; that if we earn more, we might lose connection with the people we care about—or worse, be seen as someone we are not. This guilt and these uncomfortable feelings lead us to play small.

So, we keep our comments vague.

We shrink the title.

We don't mention the promotion.

We hide the win.

And not just in conversation. We skip the online post when something remarkable happens. We don't tell our extended family when we land the client, hit the bonus, or win an award. We tell ourselves it's no big deal or that we're just being low-key, but oftentimes we're avoiding discomfort. We don't want to seem like we're bragging. We're afraid of the eye roll, the silence, or the subtle shift in someone's tone.

So, we stay quiet.

We internalize the message that success is something to manage rather than celebrate. Sometimes, we even postpone our own joy, promising ourselves that we'll feel good later—after the next milestone, the next raise, the next big win. "Once I really make it, then I'll celebrate. Then I'll breathe." But the marker of enough keeps shifting, and we continue trying to be palatable, even when we have earned something truly worth being proud of.

But when we hide our wins, we not only deny ourselves a moment of joy; we also reinforce the belief that success is dangerous, visibility is risky, and achievement comes with an emotional cost.

And over time, this silence builds resentment. Not because other people don't celebrate us, but because we never gave them the chance.

We never invited them in.

We never let ourselves feel it fully.

We never realized how much of a difference hearing the applause makes.

You don't have to shout your wins from the rooftops if that's not your style. But you do deserve to celebrate them. To own them. To share them with people who will cheer you on.

Because the more we normalize women succeeding and being seen in that success, the more we chip away at the guilt that has been passed down for generations.

In April 2025, while writing this very book, I received the prestigious Hans Severiens Award from the Angel Capital Association. This award is presented annually to one individual who has made a significant contribution to angel investing. It is akin to a lifetime achievement award—minus the tuxedos and dramatic orchestral music.

And still, I had a hard time celebrating it.

Mind you, I had already written the paragraphs above about women downplaying their wins, literally just wrote them, and yet there I was, shrinking my own win. The irony wasn't lost on me.

I pushed myself to share it online and off, and when I did, people responded with so much warmth and kindness. But doing so felt vulnerable. I had this brief, irrational fear that someone might say, "Wow, someone's full of herself today." (No one did.)

The experience made me think: We have zero trouble celebrating the people we care about. When a friend gets promoted or a niece gets into her dream school, we go full confetti cannon—texts, emojis, cake, the works. But when it's our turn? We hesitate. We mumble something vague like, "Oh, it was nothing," and quickly change the subject. At least, I did.

At first, I didn't feel comfortable celebrating, but I realized I am part of the problem here as well. By shrinking my own wins, I'm sending a message to those around me, especially other women, that success should be hidden. That pride should be managed.

I need to celebrate. Not just for me, but so others feel empowered to do the same.

Not Knowing Enough

Money guilt can be sneaky because it doesn't always feel like guilt. It often appears as hesitation, avoidance, or even indifference.

You might say, "I'm just not a money person," or "That's not really my thing." But underneath those casual comments is often something deeper: the belief that if you didn't learn it by now, it's too late, or worse, that it's not worth the effort. And so, you avoid it. You outsource it. You let someone else take the lead.

I once spoke with a woman, let's call her Erin, who owns a highly successful business. She's smart, respected, driven, and undeniably accomplished. But when the topic of money came up,

The Quiet Grip of Money Guilt

she smiled and said, "Oh, I let my finance guy handle all that. I don't like to admit it, but I really don't know what I'm doing when it comes to money. I just ... don't think I'm good at it, so I leave it to him."

She said it casually, like it was no big deal. But when I asked more, she admitted she didn't really know much about either her business finances or her personal ones. She trusted others to make the decisions and avoided looking too closely herself.

Erin isn't lazy. She isn't incapable. She has built something extraordinary. But somewhere along the way, she internalized the belief that she couldn't or shouldn't be the one in control when it came to money. That someone else was better equipped to handle it. That she didn't need to learn more, because the discomfort of admitting she didn't know felt more acceptable than the potential benefits of learning.

That's not incompetence. That's conditioning.

Most women weren't taught how to build financial confidence. We were taught to be responsible, to save, and to spend wisely. But confidence doesn't grow from being careful; it grows from understanding, ownership, and the process of trying, failing, and figuring things out.

Erin's story isn't uncommon. Many high-achieving, brilliant women relinquish their financial agency because they have convinced themselves they are not suited for it.

But you aren't behind.

You aren't broken.

You are simply carrying beliefs that were never yours to begin with.

It's not your fault if no one taught you. However, it is within your power to start learning now, without shame, without judgment, and without surrendering your power in the process.

Recognizing How Guilt Shows Up

You have just seen a handful of ways money guilt and playing small can show up—in spending, in earning, in staying quiet, in deferring to others, and in feeling like you're not qualified to take the lead.

Perhaps some of these examples hit close to home. Maybe they made you think of moments in your own life when you hesitated, minimized, or quietly handed over control, not because you couldn't handle the situation, but because you believed you weren't supposed to.

The work begins by recognizing your own patterns. Just with awareness. Not with blame. Not with shame. Because guilt thrives in silence. But the moment you start to name it, you take away its power.

Money guilt can sound like practicality, appear as humility, and feel like responsibility. But if you start paying close attention, you'll begin to notice the subtle ways guilt might be driving your decisions. You must pay attention not just to what you do with money, but also how you feel when you're doing it.

Start by noticing your reactions when you make a purchase, set a boundary, talk about money, or avoid a decision altogether. What's happening in your body? In your self-talk? Are you defending the choice to yourself before anyone has even questioned it? Do you feel tense, uneasy, or apologetic, even if the action was objectively reasonable?

Also, pay attention to your patterns. Are there certain situations where you consistently shrink, delay, or defer? Are there people around whom you often feel the need to justify or downplay your financial decisions? Or any decisions for that matter?

You are not looking for a perfect framework. Stop thinking it even exists. Instead, you are looking for clues.

This isn't about analyzing every transaction or overthinking every financial choice. It's about creating a bit more awareness, a little more space, and a lot more honesty.

Because when you recognize guilt for what it is—not truth, not instinct, but an old emotional reflex—you finally give yourself the power to do something different.

When Guilt May Be Useful

Before we can release guilt, we need to understand where it comes from. Not all discomfort related to money is inherited. Sometimes, what feels like guilt is actually your internal compass signaling a misalignment between your actions and your values. The key is learning to distinguish between helpful guilt and distracting guilt.

Inherited guilt often whispers phrases like *I don't deserve this* or *What will people think?* It is rooted in outdated messaging and a fear of judgment. It centers on playing small to remain safe, although in reality, it seldom protects you.

Values-based discomfort sounds different. It might show up as *This doesn't feel aligned*, or *This isn't where I want my money going right now*. It's less emotional and more rational, like your inner guidance system providing useful feedback.

When money decisions feel uncomfortable, ask yourself what you are really responding to. Are you concerned about other people's opinions? Or are you out of tune with your own values? A helpful trick is to remove yourself from the equation—if you'd encourage a friend to move forward despite your own hesitation, it's likely inherited guilt holding you back.

Guilt arising from conditioning feels personal and is often intertwined with shame, frequently linked to others' opinions. In contrast, guilt stemming from misalignment feels more like a gentle nudge, a reminder to realign with what truly matters.

That's why some discomfort is worth paying attention to. If your spending does not align with your values, your goals, or your reality, this misalignment can signal a need to pause and reassess. You're not bad for wanting something, but you might need to check whether you are being intentional or reactive.

So next time discomfort arises, pause and get curious. Ask yourself: Is this about your values, or is it about someone else's expectations? Let that clarity guide your next move.

Because the goal isn't to eliminate all discomfort—it's to make decisions from a place of self-trust. And you are far more capable than your guilt allows you to believe.

Begin Shifting Money Guilt

Once you start noticing when guilt shows up, the next step isn't to fix it, fight it, or push it away. Instead, pause. Name it. And remind yourself that guilt doesn't always mean you are doing something wrong.

Often, it simply means you are doing something different—something that stretches beyond what you were taught to consider acceptable.

Of course, this isn't about justifying every impulse. We are not talking about the guilt you feel after blowing your budget on a whim.

We are talking about the guilt that creeps in around thoughtful, reasonable choices. Choices that make sense for your life but feel emotionally too much because of what you have been taught to believe. That's inherited guilt. And that's worth unraveling.

Here are a few ways to start loosening inherited guilt's grip:

1. Name It When It Shows Up

The moment you catch yourself thinking, *I shouldn't be spending this*, or *I don't really deserve that*, stop and say either out loud or in your head, "That's guilt talking." It sounds simple, but naming it takes it out of the shadows and puts you back in the driver's seat. You shift from reacting to responding.

2. Ask: Is This Mine? Or Was This Given to Me?

Think back to the reflection questions from Chapter Two. Remember, much of our guilt isn't actually ours; it's inherited from our families, cultures, and industries. When you catch a guilt response, ask yourself:

- Where did this belief come from?
- Is it still true for me?
- Do I want to keep it?

This small pause can create space between the old story and your current reality.

3. Reframe the Moment

Try shifting from "I feel bad spending this money" to:

- "I'm choosing to invest in something that supports me."
- "I'm choosing to align my actions with my values and needs."
- "I'm allowed to enjoy the money I've earned."

You don't need to fake confidence. Just tell yourself a truer story. One rooted in intention, not fear.

4. Take One Small Action, even if the Guilt is Still There

Guilt doesn't always disappear immediately, and that's okay.
Sometimes, the most powerful thing you can do is to act anyway.
Spend the money. Ask the question. Set the boundary. Celebrate the win.
Let the nervousness ride shotgun as you take the wheel.

You don't have to completely clear all your guilt before moving forward.

You just need to stop letting it steer.

Guilt is sticky. It's subtle. And for many women, it's been there for so long, it feels like a personality trait, rather than what it truly is—conditioning.

But here's what matters most: You are not your guilt. You are the one noticing it, naming it, questioning it. That makes you powerful.

You don't have to get everything right. You don't need to be perfectly confident, completely clear, or guilt-free to make progress. You simply need to stay in the practice of awareness, of choosing, of returning to what's true for you.

Every time you recognize guilt and still move in the direction of what you value, you are rewriting the script—for yourself and for those who follow.

Reflection Questions

When was the last time I felt uncomfortable spending money on myself, even though I could afford it?

_____

_____

_____

_____

_____

_____

_____

The Quiet Grip of Money Guilt

When have I downplayed a success, raise, or opportunity to avoid making someone else uncomfortable? Was there a time when I stood my ground and achieved a positive outcome?

_____

_____

_____

_____

_____

What are five things I could get rid of right now that no longer serve me?

_____

_____

_____

_____

_____

What would I do differently if I didn't feel the need to explain, apologize, or minimize myself?

_____

_____

_____

_____

_____

Chapter Four

The Ripple Effect of Playing Small

Part of Izzy's optimistic attitude is reflected in a saying he has about people. He says, "People don't wake up in the morning and say to themselves, 'I'm going to be a jerk today.'" He usually says this when I'm injecting some commentary about someone or something.

And in the same spirit, I'd add, "Most people don't wake up and say, 'Today, I'm going to play small.'"

We don't consciously think about playing small, but sometimes we do it. Not because we lack ambition or because we're weak, confused, or unsure of what we want. We play small in many areas of our lives beyond money, such as relationships, careers, or even taking up space in a room. We also hold back from claiming other forms of wealth: time, rest, joy, creativity, and connection. These are all valuable currencies, yet we often treat them as optional or indulgent. We play small because it has been ingrained in our brains. Somewhere along the way, we

The Ripple Effect of Playing Small

learned that shrinking is safer than standing tall, and that it's more polite to minimize ourselves than to risk being too much.

And the thing about playing small is—it's quiet.

It doesn't make a scene.

It often seems reasonable to stay humble and wait until you're "ready."

It's in the small, automatic behaviors, like prefacing a perfectly smart idea with, "This might be dumb, but…"

And it's also in the higher-stakes choices, like sitting in a meeting and hearing a recommendation that doesn't feel aligned with the situation and still remaining silent out of fear of sounding uninformed.

Playing small doesn't always look like fear.

Sometimes it looks like politeness.

Like being "reasonable."

Like waiting for your turn.

It can appear in various aspects of your life: career, relationships, finances, and friendships. It is present in the boardroom and at the dinner table in how you speak about yourself, ask for what you need, or determine what you allow yourself to want.

But what you're really doing is holding back. Hesitating. Making yourself smaller to stay within your comfort zone or someone else's.

You might relate to some of the stories here.

Carmen ran into a friend. "Your hair looks amazing today!" her friend said.

Without missing a beat, Carmen waved it off. "Ugh, it's so thin, I can't get it to do anything."

It was automatic. She didn't even pause to consider saying thank you. The compliment made her squirm slightly, as if it drew too much attention. So, she downplayed it, just to make it feel smaller.

It wasn't about the hair. It rarely is.

Her downplaying stemmed from discomfort with being noticed, even in something as simple as a kind word from a friend.

Carmen had learned that accepting praise without minimizing it felt too bold. So, instead of embracing it, she deflected it.

Tasha had just started seeing someone. They had been out a few times, and things were going well—but she found herself constantly defaulting to whatever he suggested.

When he asked where she wanted to go for dinner, she had a favorite spot in mind, but she smiled and said, "Whatever you feel like!"

She didn't want to seem picky.

She wanted to be easygoing, agreeable, and low-maintenance.

She later confessed to a friend that this was precisely the moment she should have spoken up, because she wasn't just making a dinner choice; she was setting a tone.

By playing it flexible, she was sending a message: I don't have strong preferences; I'll go along with whatever.

And that wasn't true.

Tasha had opinions, desires, and a clear point of view.

But she was afraid that expressing those feelings too soon might rock the boat. So she stayed quiet. Even though the long-term cost of remaining silent was much greater than choosing the wrong restaurant.

Amanda instinctively said, "I'm sorry," when someone bumped into her while walking past her in a coffee shop.

She wasn't in the way. She hadn't done anything wrong.

But the words came out before she even thought about them.

Later that day, she realized she had done it again. This time, during a Zoom meeting, she unmuted herself and said, "Sorry, just one quick thing…" before offering a thoughtful, on-point suggestion.

And again, when she asked a question at the store.

And again, when she needed help at work.

It hit her: She was apologizing for existing. For speaking. For taking up space.

Amanda had been trained to soften herself. To avoid appearing too direct, too assertive, too confident. "Sorry" wasn't an expression of remorse. It was a reflex. A preemptive buffer. A way to make herself smaller so no one else would feel uncomfortable.

But every unnecessary "I'm sorry" subtly reinforced the idea that she was somehow in the way. That she needed to justify her presence. That her thoughts, her questions, her time, all came with an asterisk.

Amanda began to wonder:

What would it feel like to say, "Excuse me," or "Thanks for waiting"?

What would it feel like to show up without an apology?

What would it feel like to truly express what I really think?

Because she wasn't actually sorry. She was simply conditioned to behave as if she were.

Maureen sat in the quarterly review meeting, watching her male colleague present a new marketing strategy she had developed for a client.

She had shared the framework with him weeks earlier when he had asked for her help. Now, he was walking through her ideas, the research, the implementation plan, and even the specific language she had crafted—without a single mention of her contribution.

Maureen felt her stomach tighten. She knew she should speak up and claim her part in the work. A simple, "I'm glad the framework we developed together is resonating," would have been enough.

But the words stayed stuck in her throat.

What if it seemed petty? What if she misjudged how much was actually hers versus how much was his refinement of her ideas? What if speaking up made her appear to be a credit-grabber rather than a team player?

So she sat quietly, taking notes on her own strategy as it was presented by someone else, telling herself she'd address it later. But later never came. By the next meeting, the strategy was simply known as his.

Maureen had exchanged recognition for the appearance of collaboration. She had opted for behind-the-scenes contributions instead of visible leadership. In making that choice, a part of her professional identity diminished.

This chapter explores the various ways women impede their progress, not only financially but also in other aspects of life, not due to failure or insecurity, but from habits, fear, or learned self-protection. We will explore how these behaviors manifest in daily life, what the actual costs involved are, and how to begin strengthening the resolve to move forward.

You don't need to transition from quiet to bold overnight. However, you must stop waiting for someone else to give you permission. This is your life. You need to own it—fully.

Why Do We Do This?

You have just read the stories of how playing small appears in everyday life. How it hides behind politeness, passivity, and self-censorship. Perhaps you recognized aspects of yourself in these stories. Not because you are incapable, but because this is what many of us have been taught that it's safer to stay small, easier to conform, and more acceptable to downplay ourselves than to risk taking up space.

So, where does this pattern come from?

Why is it so deeply ingrained?

And what's really driving the hesitation to step forward, speak up, and show up fully?

Most women don't play small because they lack ability, but because they've been rewarded for playing small. Encouraged. Conditioned. Trained.

From a young age, many of us absorbed the message—whether it was spoken aloud or merely modeled quietly—that it's safer to be liked than to stand out. This message suggests that staying agreeable helps maintain harmony. It implies that

The Ripple Effect of Playing Small

confidence can be seen as arrogance, and ambition might rub people the wrong way.

Over time, those lessons take hold. You begin to pull back, you have something to say, but being bold starts to feel risky. You hesitate to be direct, worried it will come across as rude. You quiet your voice, because you've learned that being accepted often comes at the cost of being fully seen.

In many cases, these were not only social beliefs but also emotional survival strategies. Perhaps speaking up in your family meant being shut down. Maybe questioning authority at school labeled you as problematic. Perhaps being easy, helpful, or accommodating got you praise, rather than pushing back for what you wanted.

Meanwhile, boys were often encouraged to be assertive, speak up, and take the lead. Their confidence was perceived as natural, and their ambition was expected. When boys were outspoken, they were called strong. Girls, bossy—or worse.

We shrink because it feels safer.

We play small because we've seen what happens when women don't.

Especially in leadership roles.

Women in positions of power often face a double standard: Speak up and they are labeled aggressive. Push too hard, abrasive. While decisiveness is regarded as a leadership quality in men, it is frequently perceived as threatening or unfeminine in women. Just to avoid being misunderstood, many women leaders begin to soften their approach by using disclaimers, downplaying their authority, or taking on additional emotional labor.

This isn't just about personality; it's about self-protection. It's about doing what it takes to remain likable, stay safe, and feel included. However, that sense of safety comes at a cost.

Every time you soften your voice to fit in or shrink away to avoid discomfort, you send yourself a subtle message that your place is only secure if you don't take up too much space. That pleasing others matters more than being true to yourself. That your worth is conditional on how agreeable, accommodating, or nondisruptive you can be.

Over time, that message sinks in. It begins to feel natural. Familiar. You start to believe that maybe you *are* too much. Maybe it *is* better to stay quiet. And before long, you are not only second-guessing your voice but also you are questioning whether you ever had the right to use it in the first place.

However, just because something feels familiar doesn't mean it's aligned. Change doesn't happen overnight. Awareness is the first step. Once you start noticing when and where you are shrinking, you can begin to shift—gently adjusting your words, your choices, and how you show up. Playing small isn't safety. It's just a habit. One you can break.

The Many Faces of Playing Small

It is essential to acknowledge that playing small looks different for everyone. The ways we've been conditioned to diminish ourselves, and the risks we face when we don't, differ greatly depending on our identities, backgrounds, and the environments we navigate.

For women of color, the consequences of speaking up are often more severe. While a white woman might be labeled bossy for being assertive, a Black woman risks being called aggressive or angry, stereotypes that can derail careers and relationships. The already narrow range of acceptable behavior becomes even more restricted.

Michelle, a Black marketing director at a tech company, noticed this disparity through her own experiences. When she confidently presented ideas in meetings, she observed discomfort among her colleagues. However, when her white female counterpart used the same tone and directness, she received praise for her leadership potential. Michelle often found herself adjusting her communication style: softening her delivery, prefacing her

The Ripple Effect of Playing Small

expertise, and diminishing her presence just to be heard without being dismissed.

"I realized I wasn't just battling the expectation to play small as a woman," Michelle reflected. "I was also fighting against decades of stereotypes about Black women being 'too much' in professional spaces. The cost of being perceived as aggressive felt too high, so I made myself smaller and smaller until I barely recognized my own voice."

For women from cultures that prioritize family over individual achievement, playing small may be perceived as a form of cultural respect rather than self-limitation. Western concepts of leaning in appear foreign or even selfish when compared with the emphasis on harmony, family honor, and attention avoidance.

Jaya grew up in a traditional Indian household where daughters were taught that their success should "never overshadow their brothers," and that drawing attention to their achievements was improper. Even after establishing a successful consulting practice, she found herself avoiding praise and downplaying her expertise when speaking with clients.

"In my culture, humility is a virtue," she explained. "But I had to learn the difference between healthy humility and harmful self-disparagement. The business world required me to advocate for myself in ways that felt uncomfortable, but I realized that my cultural values and professional success didn't have to be in conflict."

For LGBTQ+ women, the practice of playing small can be developed early as a survival mechanism—a way to avoid unwanted attention or rejection. This habit can persist long after the initial threat has passed.

For women with disabilities, playing small might mean not asking for accommodations, not advocating for accessibility, or minimizing their needs to avoid being seen as difficult or high maintenance. This often happens even when such support is medically necessary, making the silence even more painful.

Underneath these diverse experiences lies a universal theme: the learned behavior of making ourselves smaller to navigate a world that often punishes women for taking up space. Although the specific manifestations vary, the underlying pattern remains remarkably consistent.

It is essential to understand that recognizing these differences isn't about establishing a hierarchy of struggle. Rather, it involves acknowledging that the journey to reclaiming your voice and presence may vary depending on your starting point and the challenges you face. For some, these challenges are deeply rooted in the environments where they live or work—systems or circumstances that cannot be easily changed by mindset alone.

The goal is not to ignore these realities or pretend they don't matter or even exist. It is to understand them clearly so you can make informed choices about when and how to move forward, recognizing that courage takes different forms in different circumstances.

The Cost of Staying Small

You may have reached this point in the chapter and thought, *I don't play small*. Perhaps you tell yourself, *I'm doing fine. I'm not hiding*. But you may want to look a little closer.

Perhaps there was a promotion you didn't apply for because you felt you weren't fully qualified. An idea you held back during a meeting, only to hear someone else express it minutes later and receive the recognition. A conversation you avoided with your partner, your team, or someone close to you because you were unsure how it would be received.

These moments don't always feel like much on their own. But they add up—quietly, and consistently. And over time, they leave a mark.

Playing small may seem protective, but it comes at a price. Not only does it affect your paycheck and professional growth, but it undermines your confidence, clarity, and sense of self. Each time you shrink to feel safe, something is sacrificed. Often, it's not just one thing; it's the buildup of missed opportunities, suppressed ideas, and silenced aspirations that gradually drain your energy.

The Financial Cost

Let's start with the obvious: When you undercharge, avoid negotiating, or hold back from pursuing growth, it adds up.

You might convince yourself it's not a big deal, you'll raise your rates next time, and this offer is good enough. However, over the course of a year (or a career), those compromises compound into real dollars lost.

And it's not just about earnings. Playing small can also show up in your financial behavior. You might delay investing, hand off decisions you don't fully understand, or avoid building wealth because you've convinced yourself you're not ready. The result? You miss opportunities to grow because you hold yourself back.

The Emotional Cost

Then there's the emotional toll. When you silence yourself, hide your wins, avoid asking, or keep shrinking yourself, you begin to feel disconnected from your own power. You question whether your needs matter. You second-guess your instincts. You dull your ambition not because it's gone but because it doesn't feel welcome.

That disconnection leads to resentment, burnout, or that heavy, quiet ache that says, *I'm not fully living the life I know I'm meant for.*

The Relational Cost

Staying small doesn't just affect how you see yourself; it shapes how others see you, too.

When you consistently make yourself the backup plan, people begin to assume it's your role. You train others to expect less from you, overlook your voice, and take your flexibility for granted. While you may maintain the peace, it often comes at the cost of your authenticity.

And the longer those patterns go unchecked, the harder they become to undo.

The Generational Cost

This is where the impact deepens. The impact of playing small doesn't stop with you. Every time you hold back your voice, you're not just staying quiet; you're showing others what that looks like. You're modeling this behavior for your children, your nieces, your coworkers, and the women who look to you for cues about what's acceptable and what's possible.

You may not say out loud, "Shrink yourself to stay safe," but the way you move through the world can send that message loud and clear.

When we do not challenge this pattern, we keep it alive. We carry fear and call it responsibility. We feel guilt and confuse it with humility. We remain silent and convince ourselves it is dignity.

However, that's not the whole story.

You weren't born afraid to take up space. You weren't born questioning your right to lead, speak, or desire. You were taught that.

As we discussed in Chapter 2, we stand at a cultural crossroads. One foot in a world shaped by survival, modesty, and caution—the legacy of generations before us. And the other in a world that's urging us to step forward, to lead differently, and to live with alignment and purpose.

If we don't pause and choose intentionally, we risk carrying forward beliefs that no longer serve us or those observing us.

The Ripple Effect of Playing Small

Every choice you make with money is a declaration of the future you believe in. It's an opportunity to live in alignment with your values, to expand what's possible for yourself and others, and to show the next generation that abundance, generosity, and impact can coexist. When we use our financial power in this way, we create more than just wealth; we become the change we want to see in the world.

The Life Stage Costs

The cost of playing small compounds differently at each life stage, creating unique penalties that can be difficult to recover from later.

Women who play small in their twenties often find themselves falling behind their peers by their thirties, not because they are less capable, but because they are less visible. The projects they didn't volunteer for, the networks they didn't build, and the risks they didn't take create a gap that requires extra effort to close later.

Women who reduce their participation during their primary earning years, often coinciding with motherhood, face what some economists call the motherhood penalty. However, it's not solely about employer bias; it also involves the opportunities women forgo, the promotions they fail to pursue, and the leadership positions they persuade themselves they aren't prepared for.

Women who hold back in their fifties and beyond often bear the steepest financial costs. These are the years when earnings can be at their highest, more senior roles become available, and wealth accumulation accelerates with stock options, bonuses, and other executive compensation plans. Holding back during this stage can mean the difference between financial security and financial stress in retirement.

The tragedy is that each life stage brings its own wisdom and capability, but playing small prevents women from leveraging these strengths when they matter most.

The Workplace Amplifier

Nowhere does playing small show up more consistently or cost more than in professional environments. This includes the workplace, boardrooms, and networking spaces. These environments don't just reflect these patterns; they amplify them. Some corporate cultures and performance evaluation systems can encourage women to step forward, but others reward them for staying in the background.

A 2024 McKinsey study highlights how microaggressions and systemic biases significantly affect women in the workplace, noting that 54 percent of women experience competence-based microaggressions and 38 percent have had their expertise questioned. Microaggressions are subtle, often unintentional comments, behaviors, or exclusions, such as interrupting women during meetings or assuming traditional gender roles, that convey messages of bias or disrespect and can be verbal, behavioral, or environmental. These incidents, though individually minor, have a cumulative impact of increased stress, decreased confidence, and negative effects on engagement and career growth for the affected women. As a result, women remain underrepresented in leadership roles, holding only 29 percent of C-suite positions, with women of color making up just 7 percent. They also face barriers when advancing to higher-paying roles, resulting in ongoing career instability and disproportionate representation in lower-wage positions.[viii]

Taken together, these statistics show the ripple effect of bias. It doesn't stop at promotions or pay; it also influences the language women use every day. In meetings, women may soften their statements with qualifiers, while men amplify theirs with certainty. Some disclaimers may look like:

"I might be wrong, but . . . "
"This is probably obvious, but . . . "
"I don't know if this makes sense . . . "

The Ripple Effect of Playing Small

These qualifiers have become so automatic that many women don't even realize they are using them. Meanwhile, male colleagues state opinions as facts, interrupt without apology, and claim intellectual territory with confidence.

Women's ideas often go unnoticed because they are overlooked in workplace and professional conversations. When a woman proposes a solution, it may be ignored. However, if a man repeats the same idea twenty minutes later, it suddenly receives attention. This isn't always intentional, yet it happens quite consistently.

This pattern teaches women that having good ideas isn't enough. They must fight for their ideas. You have to repeat them. You have to claim them explicitly. However, many women, like Maureen with her idea for a new marketing strategy, have been conditioned to perceive this kind of advocacy as aggressive or self-serving. Because they often don't have a model to follow, it feels like a pioneering moment every time they stand up for themselves.

Professional advancement often occurs through informal networks—the after-work drinks, the golf outings, the casual conversations. Women face a dilemma: Should they participate, risking being perceived as neglecting family responsibilities? Or should they skip these events and miss out on the relationship-building that drives career growth?

Many women resolve this by simply opting out, convincing themselves that they don't need those connections. However, career advancement is not based on merit alone; it's also depends on visibility, sponsorship, and being remembered when opportunities arise.

Women are increasingly creating their own networking spaces. In my book *Do Good While Doing Well*, I discuss how women are discovering more of their own "golf courses" by engaging with shared interest groups, particularly those focused on investing, entrepreneurship, and professional development. These environments empower women to build meaningful professional relationships while participating in activities that align with their interests and values, rather than forcing themselves into traditional networking models that may feel uncomfortable or exclusionary.

The key is to recognize that networking doesn't have to conform to traditional expectations. It's about building genuine relationships grounded in shared values, interests, and goals.

New communication dynamics concerning visibility and presence have emerged due to the rise of remote and hybrid work following the COVID-19 pandemic. Some women have found it easier to express their voices in virtual meetings—the chat function allows contributions without interruption, and the more structured format helps level the playing field.

However, remote work has also made informal relationship-building more challenging. The casual, spontaneous conversations that foster sponsorship and advocacy are harder to come by when interactions are brief and scheduled.

A female law partner once shared an observation that stayed with me. She said that when male partners gathered casually, around the water cooler or at a firm event, they often discussed the major cases they were handling or the size of the deals they were closing. Meanwhile, many of the women talked about shoes, kids, or weekend plans. Yes, visibility matters, but even more importantly, women need to feel just as comfortable talking about the big cases they are working on. This needs to be the norm.

When people don't know what your strengths are, they can't advocate for you. If we want more seats at the table, we must show up as if we belong there. This includes sharing our achievements, highlighting our strengths, and showing our work willingly. It also means being visible in the first place and making time to connect with others. Men often carve out space for these conversations, even on busy days, while women are more likely to say they don't have time. But if we don't make space for ourselves, no one else will.

The workplace will likely always present unique challenges for women striving to balance collaboration and self-advocacy. However, understanding these patterns is the first step toward changing them and creating professional environments where stepping forward feels natural rather than risky.

Being Bold

You didn't wake up one day and decide to play small. You were conditioned to do so.

This was not your fault. It was not personal. It was generational.

But now, with awareness, comes the power of choice.

The goal isn't to pretend you are fearless. It isn't about forcing boldness or confidence in situations that still feel fragile.

The real goal is to stop shrinking yourself just to feel safe.

To stop apologizing for your voice, your strength, or your needs.

To take up space because this is your life. You deserve to live it fully.

I know what it feels like to be asked to play small. Years ago, after working at the same company for many years, I was asked to take over a department. My immediate boss valued my work and wanted me in the role. But when the formal offer came, there was a catch: I wouldn't be given the title of vice president, the very title the man before me had held. I was told I needed to earn it.

That decision wasn't my boss's; he actually fought for me. It came from higher up. In that moment, I had a choice: walk away or step in anyway. I chose to take the role. I poured my energy into leading the department, supporting the staff, and helping them achieve the goals they cared about most. Eventually, the company did give me the title. But by then, it was too late. The message had already been sent, and I realized I wasn't going to let myself keep playing by those rules.

Unapologetic Wealth

I left the company on a high note, right after the annual results came in stronger than ever before. I was proud of what I had built and clear about something more important: standing up for yourself matters—for you and as a role model for others. Along with knowing when to give your best and when to walk away, rather than shrinking yourself to fit someone else's idea of what you deserve.

I wasn't made to shrink, and neither were you. We were made to shape, contribute, and lead with presence and clarity. We were meant to show up. Fully, honestly, and without needing to explain ourselves.

The concept of cultural crossroads applies not only to money but also to leadership.

On one side is the mindset passed down to us from generations of women who had to prioritize safety and survival above all else. They navigated a world with fewer options, fewer rights, and greater risks associated with speaking up. On the other side is a vastly evolved world offering more opportunities, autonomy, and access than ever before. Yet many of us still live by the old-world rules.

You can honor the wisdom of those who came before you while refusing to be limited by their constraints. You can be grateful for their sacrifices while claiming the freedoms they fought to create. You can respect the lessons of the past while creating new ones for the future.

Notice when you are about to apologize for having an opinion. Catch yourself before you deflect a compliment. Speak up in that meeting. Share your ideas without a disclaimer. Ask for what you need without extensive justification.

These aren't dramatic gestures—they are micro-revolutions; small acts of reclaiming space that, over time, reshape not just how others see you but also how you see yourself.

In the documentary *Show Her the Money*, where I had the privilege of serving as an associate producer, Dawn Lafreeda says three simple words that made waves around the world:

The Ripple Effect of Playing Small

"I like money." That statement sparked a flood of feedback. Women from different countries, backgrounds, and professions reached out to share that they had never felt safe expressing those words aloud. They had been taught to hide their desires, to downplay their ambitions, to distance themselves from wealth as if it were something improper. But hearing another woman name it—clearly and unapologetically—gave them permission to do the same.

Your ideas, your leadership, your full presence—these are not luxuries the world can do without. They are necessities. Every time you shrink to make others comfortable, you deprive the world of something it truly needs. Every time you stay silent to keep the peace, you rob others of perspectives that could make a difference.

The women watching you—your daughters, nieces, colleagues, and friends—are learning from how you navigate the world. They observe what's possible by seeing the choices you make.

Stop waiting to be ready. Stop waiting for everything to be perfect. Stop waiting for someone else to make space for you.

Make space for yourself.

The world needs women who are unafraid to be powerful, unashamed to be ambitious, and unwilling to play small just to make others comfortable.

The world needs you. All of you.

Not the diminished version. Not the apologetic version. Not the conforming version.

You.

Full-size, full-voice, fully present.

Will you continue to live by rules that no longer serve you? Or will you write new ones?

The pen is in your hand.

Exercise: Neurographic Drawing— Money, Me & My Future

The following neurographic exercise is a simple, creative way to help your nervous system relax and release tension. You can use it anytime you want to quiet your mind, reduce stress, or simply reconnect with yourself. Neurographic drawing blends art and mindfulness, engaging your brain in a way that gently shifts you from stress to a calmer, and more focused state.

If this already sounds way too woo-woo for you, that's okay. It probably means you need it even more. Worst case, you've just made some strange squiggly lines. Best case, you accidentally tricked yourself into feeling like a Zen master with a pen.

What you'll need: Paper (or use the space provided), a black pen or marker, and some colored pencils or markers (optional but adds to the fun)
Steps:

1. **Set Your Intention**

Take a few deep breaths. Place one hand on your heart. Quietly ask yourself:
What would it feel like to be at peace with money?
Or:
What would life look like if I believed I was good with money?
Don't force an answer. Just sit with the question for a moment.

2. **Draw Lines Freely**

Take your black pen and, starting anywhere on the page, draw a series of random, looping, curving lines. Let them flow across the page like a lazy river. Don't lift your pen until you feel finished—five to seven lines should be enough. Let them cross and intersect.

3. Round the Edges

Where the lines intersect, you'll see sharp angles or corners. Go in and round those corners—draw small curves over the angles, make everything feel smooth and connected, like you are creating little nodes. This process is meditative and helps integrate conflicting thoughts and emotions. You may begin to feel calmer simply by doing this.

4. Add Color (optional but really fun!)

Pick two to three colors. Let yourself fill in the shapes made by the intersecting lines. Don't overthink it—simply pick the colors you're drawn to. You can assign meanings to them (peace, abundance, clarity) or you can simply enjoy the process.

5. Reflect

Once you're done, take a moment to look at what you've created. Ask yourself:

- How do I feel now compared to before I started drawing?
- What part of the drawing stands out to me?
- If this drawing were a map of my financial journey, where would I be?

This process might seem simple, but it does something powerful—it shifts your energy and creates space for new possibilities. From here, we move toward structure and clarity.

The Ripple Effect of Playing Small

Here is an example of a neurographic drawing.

Reflection Questions

In which specific situations do you find yourself apologizing unnecessarily?

_____

_____

_____

What messages did you receive about ambition, success, and leadership while growing up?

_____

_____

_____

What opportunities have you missed in the past month/year due to not speaking up? What are your achievements?

_____

_____

_____

Who has tried to diminish you or your contributions and made you feel small? Who has been your champion?

_____

_____

_____

THE RIPPLE EFFECT OF PLAYING SMALL

What would you attempt if you knew you couldn't fail?

_____

_____

_____

Chapter Five

Shift from Playing Small to Being Bold

You have begun to do the inner work.

You've identified the patterns. You've questioned the old stories. You've begun untangling the guilt, recognized the ways you've played small, and redefined what wealth means to you.

Now comes the part that feels both exciting and terrifying: actually taking action. Insight without action keeps you stuck. Clarity without movement is just another form of waiting. You don't need more time, more confidence, or more permission. You need to move.

This chapter focuses on managing your financial life starting from where you are right now. You don't need to have everything figured out, nor do you have to do it all alone. It involves showing up intentionally, asking tough questions, pushing through resistance, saying no when something doesn't feel right, and saying yes when it does. Even if it scares you.

Advocating for yourself isn't selfish. It isn't pushy. It is responsible, mature, and long overdue for many of us.

If you have ever felt unsure or hesitant, this chapter serves as your reminder: growth begins when you take action. It's about choosing to move forward with intention, courage, and clarity, regardless of your starting point.

You Never Think It Will Happen to You

Priya, a brilliant and respected physician, found herself in an unexpected financial situation.

She met her husband, Alex, while completing her residency. He worked in finance and had already begun building substantial wealth. From the start, he managed their finances as he understood the complexities of his compensation packages, accounts, and investments. Priya allowed him to take the lead in that area. It felt like a sensible division of labor at the time—one of the chores for him to handle.

Priya assumed she had access to everything. They talked about *their* money openly. She had the cards, statements, and logins. However, she didn't realize that while she was working demanding shifts at the hospital and raising their children, Alex had opened and was actively managing accounts she didn't even know existed.

One of those accounts was used to pay for an apartment and expenses for another woman, his mistress.

When Priya discovered the truth, everything changed. The betrayal was not only emotional but also financial. As they proceeded with the divorce, Alex became increasingly controlling and secretive. He used financial jargon to confuse her, stalled on essential documents, and exaggerated the complexity and severity of the situation.

Initially, Priya felt paralyzed. She didn't know where to begin and wasn't used to asking questions about their finances. Then, something clicked. She realized she couldn't afford to stay ignorant anymore. This nightmare went beyond betrayal or heartbreak; it was about control, fairness, and protecting her future, as well as her children's.

So, she educated herself, asked for help, and gained confidence. Eventually, she was able to advocate for what was fair for herself and her children. It didn't happen overnight, but with patience and diligence, she succeeded once she stopped sitting quietly on the sidelines.

This story highlights the dangers of fully outsourcing your financial control, even to someone you love. It's a cautionary tale but also a rallying cry. Too many people believe this won't happen to them. Until it does.

When wealth or earning potential is uneven in a relationship, and you are not proactive in understanding the full picture, complications arise—especially as assets grow and financial decisions accumulate.

Letting someone else handle it might feel easier in the moment. But knowledge is protection. Clarity is power. And asking questions, even hard ones, is responsible.

Stories like Priya's highlight an important truth: You don't have to manage everything, but you must understand enough to recognize when something feels amiss.

Too many people are caught off guard by financial surprises they never anticipated: a divorce, an unexpected job loss, an unforeseen medical bill, or the passing of a loved one. These occurrences, unfortunately, are not rare. They are part of life, and the key is to be prepared. Having clarity and a plan is paramount.

You Don't Need to Wait

Danielle is a sales director at a growing startup. She is smart, organized, and excellent at her job, but when it comes to finances, she mostly stays out of it. She has never felt the need to fully engage. Her husband manages the bills, oversees the accounts, and occasionally provides her with summaries when something

Shift from Playing Small to Being Bold

important comes up. Everything seems fine, so she doesn't think much about it.

On a random Tuesday, while filling out school paperwork for one of her children, she came across a question about household finances that she couldn't answer. It was a minor issue, but it weighed heavily on her. She realized she didn't actually know where their accounts were located, how much they saved each month, or what their long-term financial plan entailed. She felt vulnerable by this realization, in a way she had not anticipated.

Danielle decided it was time to step in. At first, she felt nervous, unsure how to start the conversation without appearing mistrustful or confrontational. She wasn't even sure what questions to ask, but she couldn't keep pretending she understood more than she actually did. One evening, she sat down with her husband and said, "I know you've been handling most of this, and I appreciate it, but I need to start understanding our finances for myself. Not because I don't trust you, but because I need to trust myself as well." It wasn't easy to admit, but that honesty opened the door to a series of conversations that brought about change.

As they sat down to review their finances together, she noticed something: they were still paying a monthly fee for a software subscription that was no longer in use. It was just $9.99 a month, but the amount had accumulated over time. This small realization flipped a switch in her mind. What else might be happening that she wasn't aware of?

She began logging into the accounts, tracking their expenses, and asking new questions. She became involved by taking small steps. More than anything, she started to feel like an engaged participant in the life she was helping to build.

Now, Danielle is more than just aware of the finances; she is actively involved. The confidence and calm that came with that shift have spilled over into other areas of her life. She has started speaking up more at work and no longer second-guesses her ideas during meetings. At home, she is setting clearer boundaries around her time and energy. Even small decisions, like choosing vacation destinations or setting gift budgets, feel less stressful. When she stopped doubting herself about money, she also stopped doubting herself in other aspects of her life.

You don't need a wake-up call to start paying attention. Danielle's moment came unexpectedly, but yours doesn't have to. This. Right now. Can. Be. Your. Moment. You don't have to wait for a crisis, a life change, or someone else to bring things to light. Awareness is enough. This is your invitation to get curious, ask questions, and step into the role of an informed owner of your financial life—no emergency required.

The Gap Between Knowing and Doing

You know you need to take action. You have read the stories, understand the stakes, and are convinced in your mind. But when it's time to actually do something, log into that account, schedule that meeting, start that conversation, your body has other plans.

Maybe your heart starts racing or your palms get sweaty. You suddenly remember seventeen other things that need your attention right now. If you are like me, when avoiding something, baking a dozen or so loaves of banana bread feels absolutely necessary in these moments. Or you sit down to review your finances but find yourself inexplicably scrolling through social media, as if your phone has a mind of its own.

Don't let your brain tell you this is a sign of weakness or procrastination. This is your nervous system responding to a perceived threat. For many of us, money conversations and financial decisions trigger our fight-or-flight response, even when we rationally know there is no real danger.

Sarah, a leadership coach, describes it perfectly: "I could give a presentation to a room full of executives without breaking a sweat, but the thought of logging into my online bank account made me physically nauseous. I kept putting it off, telling myself I was too busy. But really, I felt overwhelmed by the thought of budgeting and planning for the future."

Shift from Playing Small to Being Bold

These emotional responses aren't random. They are often rooted in past experiences, family patterns, or cultural messages we absorbed long ago. Perhaps you grew up hearing, "Money doesn't grow on trees," every time you asked for something. Or you may have witnessed heated arguments about finances. Perhaps you internalized the message that "Good girls don't ask for money" or that being overly concerned about finances means being materialistic.

The first step is to notice what happens in your body as it involuntarily responds to these patterns and messages when you encounter money-related tasks.

Sometimes you may suddenly find urgent reasons to clean the house, check your email, or handle almost any other task except the financial one.

Perhaps you sit down to take action but feel frozen, unable to make even the simple decisions.

Perhaps you feel overwhelmed by too many options, or you find yourself researching endlessly without ever taking action.

You might experience headaches, have stomach knots, or feel exhausted when thinking about money.

These responses are not character flaws. They are simply information. Your body is trying to protect you from a perceived danger, even if that danger is outdated or imaginary. It's okay to feel this way. Acknowledge the feeling, maybe even thank it for trying to keep you safe and then take a small step forward anyway.

Moving Through, Not Around

You can start smaller than you think is necessary. If the idea of reviewing all your accounts feels daunting, begin with just one. Small actions build momentum and show your nervous system that you can handle more than it expects.

When you begin to feel your body panicking, try simple grounding techniques. Notice your surroundings—the temperature of the air, the sounds in the room, and the feeling of your feet on the floor. This helps you return to the present moment and exit the fight-or-flight response.

Reframe your narrative. Instead of saying, "I have to figure this out," try, "I'm learning something new." Instead of thinking, "I should already know this," try, "I'm exactly where I need to be." The story you tell yourself about your financial journey matters more than you might think.

Connect the financial action to something that matters deeply to you. It could be your children's security, your own peace of mind, or your desire to model empowerment for other women. When emotional resistance arises, remind yourself why this is important.

And remember, you don't have to do this alone. Whether it's a trusted friend, a financial advisor who makes you feel comfortable, or even a therapist who understands money anxiety, having support makes the emotional journey much more manageable.

Feeling scared or overwhelmed doesn't mean you should stop. It just shows you are human and still making progress. The women who appear confident about money? Many of them probably felt the same way when they started. They just kept going regardless.

Emotional work is part of the financial work. As you practice moving through these feelings instead of waiting for them to disappear, you'll build financial confidence and develop a deeper trust in your ability to handle whatever challenges come your way.

Building a Working Relationship with Your Money

Financial control, or agency, is about understanding every aspect of your financial situation and ensuring you are never left in the dark.

You don't need to become a financial wizard or know every investment option available. However, you do need a solid understanding of your money. This means knowing what you have, what's coming in, what's going out, and what your money is actually doing for you—or not doing. This is especially important if you have delegated financial decisions to a partner, an advisor, or even a family member; you should still maintain visibility and have a voice.

In practice, this can look like this:

- **Know what accounts and assets exist.** Checking accounts, savings, credit cards, investment accounts, retirement funds, insurance policies, house, car, art, and jewelry. Get familiar with all the accounts with positive or negative balances, as well as the assets within your family. Get a good sense of your financial picture and what protection you currently have, or don't have.
- **Understand your income, expenses, and investments.** Where does your money go each month? What are you spending, saving, and setting aside for future goals? What investments do you already have, and what are your investment goals moving forward?
- **Be clear about your debts.** Which debts are in your name? Which are shared? What are the terms, interest rates, and repayment plans? This may include mortgages, car loans, personal loans, student loans, or any other money owed.
- **Know who has access.** Who is listed on your accounts? What if your relationship or family situation changes? Are you aware of the passwords, institutions, and contacts?
- **Assess your alignment.** Are your financial behaviors, including spending, saving, and investing aligned with the goals you care about most? Or are you drifting off course?

If you're in a relationship, asking, "Are we okay this month?" does not count as a financial conversation. You should engage in deeper discussions about goals, fears, and long-term plans. Avoiding these conversations may seem polite, but it creates silence. Silence that can quickly lead to confusion or regret. It can grow into something much bigger than necessary.

If you are single or your finances are solely your responsibility, regularly review all your accounts. Don't assume everything is fine just because you haven't seen any overdraft notices this month.

If you work with a financial advisor, you should never leave a meeting feeling small or unsure. If something isn't clear, ask, "Can you explain that in simpler terms?" You have the right to ask questions, learn, and fully understand. If your advisor doesn't create space for that, it may be time to find someone who does.

Taking steps toward clarity is a powerful act. Telling yourself you'll deal with it later or when you have more time is just another way of staying stuck. Doing nothing is still doing something—it's quietly agreeing to remain in the dark. And that's not acceptable. You deserve to understand your money and have control over it. Face your finances head-on. Ask the uncomfortable questions. The sooner you do, the more peace, confidence, and authority you'll gain for your future.

Using Your Voice Around Money

Understanding your numbers is one aspect of financial agency. But discussing them? That's power in action.

And yet, this is where many women tend to freeze. We hold back from asking questions when we don't understand. We nod along in meetings even when we don't fully agree. We defer to partners or professionals because we have been conditioned to believe that discussing money is risky. We worry that we'll sound naive, make others uncomfortable, or appear greedy, demanding, or difficult.

Shift from Playing Small to Being Bold

It doesn't help that *financial professional* can refer to many different roles. A financial advisor is a broad designation. Anyone can technically call themselves one. Therefore, it is important to ask how they are compensated and what licenses they hold. A Certified Financial Planner (CFP) has met rigorous standards of education, certification, and ethical practice, and is trained to consider the full picture of your financial life. An insurance agent, on the other hand, is licensed to sell insurance products, which may or may not align with your broader financial goals. None of these roles are inherently good or bad, but it is important to understand that you know your financial service providers, their expertise, and the motivations behind their recommendations.

Because not knowing and silence can be expensive.

If you don't ask about fees, you might end up overpaying through hidden charges on investments, account maintenance, and advisory costs—all quietly chipping away at your returns. Over time, these small percentages can add up to thousands of dollars.

If you don't question a financial plan, you might end up committing to strategies misaligned with your goals/values or investing in products with the fees that benefit someone else. A good plan should be tailored specifically to your life, not just a generic model.

If you avoid discussions about shared finances, you might unknowingly build a future based on completely different assumptions, such as early retirement for one partner and paying off debt on a different timeline for the other. Honest conversations now can prevent a lot of confusion and conflict later.

Speaking up doesn't require having all the answers. It simply requires curiosity and a willingness to be seen. You can ask, "Can we review this again?" or "What would this look like in six months?" You can say, "I'd like to think about this before deciding," or "This doesn't sit right with me. Can we explore additional options?"

These phrases show that you are paying attention and seeking clarity.

In addition to speaking up, you should negotiate. If you don't, you might leave money on the table. Whether it's a higher salary, better benefits, or perks like stipends, training, or flexible hours, making your life easier and more sustainable, remember that the initial offer is often just a starting point.

Take Maya, for example. She was being considered for a promotion and was told it would come with additional compensation. Rather than just nodding and moving on, she asked a simple but powerful question: "Can you walk me through what that means, exactly?"

That one question opened the door to a much more meaningful conversation. She discovered she could negotiate not just her salary but also her schedule and support for her professional growth. Instead of working in the office five days a week, she was allowed to choose three days to come in, working remotely for the remaining hours as long as she completed her work. Additionally, she secured a stipend to help her earn a certification, after which she would qualify for another raise.

None of it would have been offered upfront. It all became possible because Maya asked.

Clarity is the foundation of building trust. Trust in yourself, trust in your partners or advisors if you have them, and trust in the decisions you make.

The more you practice expressing your thoughts, asking questions, or seeking clarifications, the easier it becomes. Financial agency develops into a skill, and you are allowed to practice it, imperfectly, awkwardly, and out loud.

Handling the Pushback

Talking about money doesn't always go smoothly. Sometimes, those around you—whether partners, advisors, or family—aren't happy about your new focus on finances. They might brush off

Shift from Playing Small to Being Bold

your questions, make you feel silly for asking, or even actively oppose your involvement.

This resistance often reveals more about them than about you.

A partner who becomes defensive when you ask about shared accounts might be hiding something, or they might just feel uneasy about change. A financial advisor who patronizes you or uses jargon to dismiss your concerns instead of protecting your interests may be shielding themselves from accountability. A family member who rolls their eyes when you ask about estate planning might feel threatened by your growing confidence.

Jennifer experienced this firsthand when she began showing more interest in the family's investment portfolio. Her husband, who had managed their finances for years, grew increasingly irritated by her questions. "You never cared about this stuff before," he would say. "Why are you suddenly so worried about everything?"

But Jennifer didn't back down. She understood that his discomfort wasn't her responsibility to manage. "I'm not worried," she told him. "I'm interested. And I'm allowed to be interested in our financial future."

When you face pushback, remember: Your desire to understand your money is reasonable and responsible, not difficult, demanding, or distrustful.

If someone in your life makes you feel small for asking questions about money, consider it a valuable signal. Good partners, advisors, and family members want you to be informed and engaged. They welcome your questions because they care about your confidence and peace of mind.

And whoever you may be talking to or working with, don't let them assume your level of expertise, just as you shouldn't assume theirs. A retired woman I know was reminded of this when she met her late father's longtime financial advisor. She casually mentioned her involvement with a local angel investing group. He raised an eyebrow and said, "Isn't that just a bunch of rich guys investing in start-ups?" Then came the real kicker—he added, "Are you doing admin work for them?" The assumption was clear and utterly wrong. He couldn't imagine that she was an active investor making decisions, writing checks, and supporting entrepreneurs. It stung, but she didn't let it shake her. She made sure to inform him she was an active investor and a member of the board of directors. His limited view had nothing to do with her ability or experience but everything to do with his own outdated assumptions.

Don't let someone else's discomfort or ignorance inhibit you from making informed, empowered decisions. You have every right to understand, question, and take ownership of every aspect of your life, including your financial life.

The Myth of Ready

One of the biggest roadblocks to financial progress? Waiting until you feel ready.

We tell ourselves we will take action once we know more, once we feel more confident, and have everything perfectly aligned. But being *ready* is often just another word for being afraid. It's our internalized storytelling that tells us we need to be perfectly prepared before we're allowed to act. And this mindset holds us back far more than we realize.

Women, in particular, have been conditioned to wait until they are 100 percent qualified before raising their hands, speaking up, or making a move. There's even a well-known example from corporate hiring that illustrates this: if a job lists five qualifications, a woman might have four and still hesitate to apply, thinking she's not quite ready. In contrast, a man might have only one and apply with full confidence. Men consistently invest in themselves, and they view any sign of success as a direct correlation of that investment.

This comes from generations of conditioning.

Shift from Playing Small to Being Bold

Men are often trained to be bold, take risks, and believe they'll figure it out as they go. In contrast, women are taught to be careful, thorough, and modest. While we may overprepare, overresearch, or overthink, opportunities can slip away. That gap between knowledge and action? It costs us time, money, and momentum.

Lena has always been curious about investing, but whenever she thinks about starting, she feels overwhelmed. Index funds, exchange-traded funds (ETFs), capital gains—all seem like a foreign language to her. She decided to wait until she has more time to take a course, save up more, or simply "think it through."

Then one afternoon over coffee, a friend mentioned that she had been investing regularly since her mid-twenties and had already built up a solid portfolio by the age of thirty. Lena was stunned, not because she discovered her friend was some financial genius but because she realized they had both started in the same place. The only difference was that her friend had taken action while she had not.

That was the wake-up call Lena needed.

That same week, she opened a brokerage account and invested her first few hundred dollars. It wasn't much, but it was movement. She made herself a simple promise: she would contribute a minimum percentage from each paycheck, no matter what.

That small step gave her something she didn't expect—momentum. She began reading more, asking questions, and gradually growing both her account and her confidence. She didn't need a finance degree. She just needed to start.

Lena no longer waited to feel ready. She took action, and that made her ready.

You can do the same.

You don't need to have everything laid out in detail to ask a question.

You don't need to reach a specific income level to start investing small amounts.

You don't need to have everything figured out to begin figuring it out.

There are no prerequisites, but the results can be life changing. What feels uncertain now won't always feel that way.

Progress only happens when you move.

You don't need to overhaul your entire financial life overnight. You don't have to wait for a moment when you magically feel more capable, confident, or prepared. What you need is to begin. Gently, imperfectly, but intentionally, with the understanding that clarity comes from doing, not from waiting.

Perhaps that means finally sitting down with your partner for the frank money conversation you've been avoiding. Perhaps it means researching questions you've been curious about. Perhaps it means opening the account you've been putting off until you have time. The point isn't where you start—it's that you start and boost your confidence by knowing you are someone who takes action.

You are already capable of making smart, aligned decisions. You are allowed to understand your money, to ask for more, and to change what isn't working. You can build a relationship with your money that reflects the life you want, not the fears you have inherited.

Yes, you are doing this for yourself, but you are also doing it for every woman who comes after you. Remember, we are standing at a cultural crossroads where the limitations of the past meet the possibilities of the future. Every time you take action, ask a question, or claim your space, you model a new way forward—and give the next generation permission to do the same.

You are now reimagining what wealth means to you. It might not always be comfortable, but it will be worth it. The more you align your actions with your values, the more your financial life will begin to feel truly your own. Surprisingly, you may even find that more money starts flowing in your direction.

Shift from Playing Small to Being Bold

Exercise: Reflection and Connection

Changing your relationship with money starts with noticing it and sensing it in your thoughts, behaviors, and emotional reactions. Most of us have unconscious patterns around money that operate in the background: a wave of guilt after spending, a feeling of panic before checking an account balance, an urge to control every dollar, or a habit of avoiding money altogether.

I first began thinking about the power of pausing and connecting to the present moment after reading Barbara Huson's *Rewire for Wealth*. She explains how to rewire your brain for financial success by shifting your neural pathways. Her approach resonated with me so deeply that I invited her to be a guest on *The Angel Next Door* podcast. (You can find it on my website or wherever you listen to podcasts.)

Barbara's work inspired these Reflection and Connection exercises, which can help you create a stronger link between the life you want and how you use your money. The exercises provide a simple approach to reflect on what's happening in the moment and take intentional steps that align your financial choices with your values.

Use this exercise whenever you feel stuck, reactive, anxious, or unsure about a financial decision. It's a tool for transforming unconscious habits into conscious choices, and that's where lasting change begins.

Reflection

Pause and notice what's really happening, both emotionally and physically, when you feel stuck, anxious, or unsure about a financial decision. Money anxiety often arrives without an invitation—tight chest, racing thoughts, a pit in your stomach, or the urge to fix or flee. Notice what's going on beneath the surface.

Turn inward and listen. Reflect on how you feel.

Ask yourself:

- What am I feeling right now—fear, shame, guilt, overwhelm?
- Where do I feel it in my body?
- What was the moment that triggered this feeling?
- Am I reacting to something in the present, or am I carrying something from the past?

These questions can become your guide through the emotions you're experiencing.

- You might journal about it.
- You might sit quietly with it.
- You might just hold it in your mind as you go about your day.

For some, a grounding exercise can be helpful.

Grounding Practice: Ninety-Second Reset

When you notice feelings of anxiety, fear, or stress, try this simple practice to return to the present moment before moving on to reflection.

Step 1: Get into your body

Plant your feet flat on the floor. If you're sitting, let your hands rest in your lap or on the table. Feel the weight of your body supported by the chair beneath you.

Step 2: Breathe in patterns

Take a deep breath in through your nose for a count of four...

Hold it for four seconds…
Breathe out slowly through your mouth for a count of six.
Do this three times.

Step 3: Name what's real, right now

Gently name what you notice:
One thing you see
One thing you hear
One thing you physically feel

This brings you back to this moment, not the panic of what-ifs or the burden of old financial stories.

Take a few moments to just be here.

Connection

Come back to what matters. Reconnect yourself to your values, your power to move forward with intention, and take your next right step.

This isn't about solving everything or snapping out of it. It's about choosing one small action that helps you move ahead.

Ask yourself:

- How can I respond in a way that honors both my values and my capacity right now?
- What's one thing I can do to support the version of me I'm becoming?
- In this moment, is there a way I can honor my values, even in a small way? This might look like:
    o Checking your account balance without judgment.
    o Taking a walk instead of doomscrolling.
    o Writing down one belief you're ready to change.

Or perhaps your next step is to pause longer. That's valid too.

Connection doesn't always require action. Sometimes, it means stillness with purpose.

But when you are ready, reconnect with your intention. Choose a step that feels aligned with the life you are trying to create.

You don't need to get it perfect. You just need to get connected.

Chapter Six

Honor the Past, Reshape the Future

We all inherit money patterns long before the day we actually inherit money.

Some people learn early that money can be unpredictable. Here one day, gone the next. So, they approach it with fear and doubt. Others are taught to keep it tightly secured, never fully trusting that there will be enough. And some grow up believing that financial security means avoiding all risks, while others swing in the opposite direction, spending freely and rarely considering the long-term consequences.

These aren't conscious lessons. No parent sits their child down and says, "Let me teach you to be anxious about money for the rest of your life." Instead, these patterns get passed down through moments like watching a parent's face when bills arrive, hearing whispered conversations about making ends meet, and feeling the tension when unexpected expenses pop up.

By the time we reach adulthood and make our own financial decisions, these patterns become so deeply ingrained that we no longer recognize them as patterns. They simply feel like truth. Like the way things are. Like the way we are.

This chapter explores how to recognize money patterns and use awareness to shift them. It explains how money habits take root, how they play out in real life, and how people notice and change them—moving closer to using money as a tool to build the life they actually want.

Opening Space for Something New

These stories offer real examples of that journey, starting with Emily's.

"This can't be right," David muttered, shuffling through a stack of bank statements with shaking hands. The numbers didn't add up, not in his favor, anyway.

"It's right," Sarah shot back, her voice edged with a bitter laugh. "We spent it. It's gone."

David slammed his fist on the table. "A million dollars, Sarah! A million!"

"Jet skis, vacations, furniture, a car for you, a car for me…" she listed, her voice growing quieter with each word. "And your drinking. Let's not forget that."

"We need to tell the girls," she said, avoiding his glare. "We're selling the house. We're moving back into an apartment. Back to where we were."

Before the money, the million dollars, their lives had been a waiting game.

David's hunting accident had taken everything from them—his ability to work, their home, and their stability. Just like that, their lives had changed. Their only hope lay in a lawsuit against the manufacturer of the equipment he had been using. The case dragged on for six years, with the family hanging by a thread of hope for the settlement money.

And when the check finally arrived, all one million dollars of it, it seemed like salvation.

A big house followed. New clothes. Expensive meals. The constant weight of worry was lifted from their shoulders.

But money had never been the problem.

David still drank. Sarah still resented his drinking. The marriage was still strained. Natalie, their oldest daughter, was sick, and her medical bills were still an ever-present burden. And Emily, the youngest, was watching it all unfold, trying to make sense of it.

The money was a distraction; a whirlwind of spending and indulgence that made them feel invincible—while it lasted.

Eventually, it was gone.

Emily had never forgotten the day her mother told them they were moving again. They couldn't afford to keep the house, the new furniture, or anything else they had bought during their brief period of luxury.

"Are we poor again?" she had asked, the words sticking in her throat.

David swallowed hard and nodded. "Yeah, kid. We're poor again."

It was in that moment that Emily learned something deeply damaging: money is unpredictable. It could be there one day and gone the next. And when it disappeared, it took everything with it.

For a long time afterward, Emily didn't think much about the past. She was smart. She got into one of the best private colleges in the country. She would do things differently. She would make something of herself. She just had to pay her dues first. That was the lesson she had internalized. Struggle came before success. She believed that if she worked hard and suffered through the debt, the reward would come.

So, she signed the student loan papers, starting with her undergraduate studies and continuing through to earning a PhD. Every semester, she signed again. She barely glanced at the totals because it didn't seem to matter. She was confident she would make good money someday. She had to. By the time she became Dr. Emily, she owed tens of thousands of dollars.

Her first job paid well, but not enough to significantly reduce her loans after covering rent and basic expenses. Like her parents, she had spent money she didn't have, thinking a big payday was in her future. The feast-or-famine pattern she inherited from her parents remained deeply ingrained in her life even now.

She leased a nice car. She used credit to buy not just her everyday living expenses but for occasional treats, telling herself she was investing in herself. She dined out. She traveled. She justified it all, because one day soon, she'd have plenty of money to cover it.

But no settlement check waited for her this time. And she was drowning.

Then came the moment that began to change things.

Emily and her roommate sold their condo and made a good profit. They had bought it in their late twenties when it hadn't felt like a financial move, just a way to stop wasting money on rent.

And for the first time, Emily felt something new.

Control.

The condo sale wasn't a matter of luck. It wasn't a gamble or a windfall—it was the result of a calculated decision. A steady, responsible financial choice that paid off in a way that seemed intentional. For the first time, she realized she no longer wanted to chase a big win. She didn't want to live paycheck to paycheck, waiting for some event to finally make her financially stable. She recognized the pattern and wanted to break the cycle. She wanted consistency. Security. A plan.

So she made one. She sat down with a notebook and wrote at the top of the page: MONEY SHOULD BE CONSISTENT, NOT A GAMBLE. Underneath that, she listed everything she wanted to change:

1. Pay off my debt. All of it. No more pretending it will disappear on its own.

2. Stop relying on credit cards. They aren't temporary money. They are traps designed to get you to keep adding to an existing balance. It's harder to add on to a card with a zero balance.
3. Build financial security with intention, not desperation.
4. Own property again, but on my own terms.

She began tracking her spending, cutting out unnecessary expenses, not to suffer but to gain control. During her work as a PhD, she met many people who supported her vision and passion for a world with better health care. One of these kind souls gave Emily a place to live rent-free for six months to get ahead with paying off that student loan debt. She wasn't waiting for a miracle anymore. She was done paying her dues, and she very clearly recognized the pattern she was ready to break. She was done waiting for the moment when money would magically fix everything. This time, she was determined to fix it herself.

Emily didn't wake up one day and decide to get her financial life in order. Her transition from chasing windfalls to building intentional wealth was gradual and deeply personal. It involved unpacking more than just her spending habits — it meant confronting the old money beliefs she had inherited. Growing up, she observed her parents swing between viewing money as a lifeline and as a looming disaster.

It was never just a tool.

And that had left a lasting mark.

Her story is a powerful reminder that we all carry money stories that started long before earning our first paycheck. These early scripts can quietly influence our decisions for years, until we pause long enough to question them. That's what Emily did. And that's when things began to change; she refused to continue following the pattern any longer.

Rewriting her money story wasn't about shame or blame. It was about awareness and then intention. Her journey from confusion to clarity is something many of us can relate to. Because when we begin to ask, "Does this old belief still serve me?" we open space for something new.

Figuring Out the Lessons from the Past

Emily's story is not unique. While writing this book, I spoke to many people about money, and almost everyone had a story to share: patterns often shaped by childhood or early life experiences. Some of these narratives serve as cautionary tales; some highlight interesting wins, while others reveal valuable lessons. You may even see your own mindset reflected in the stories throughout these pages. Let's consider another example.

Julie was eleven the first time she filled out and tore a check from a checkbook. Not for herself—she didn't even get an allowance—but for her mom, who worked long shifts at the diner and still came home to cook dinner and sit with Julie at their small kitchen table to go through the bills.

It became their monthly ritual. Julie would line up the bills by due date, calculate what had to be paid now and what might wait a week or more, then balance the checkbook with the focus of a junior accountant. Rent, utilities, and groceries were the priorities. They were nonnegotiable. After that? Usually nothing much was left.

When Julie's friends talked about buying new clothes or the latest toy, she didn't even ask. She already knew. Not because her mom would say no, but because she had seen the numbers.

"We've got forty-seven dollars left after everything," Julie would say, pencil in hand.

Her mom would smile, tired but proud. "Good job, sweetheart. What should we do with it?"

The answer never changed: save it, because you never knew what might come next.

By middle school, Julie could stretch a dollar better than most grown-ups. She had learned early how to manage credit card minimums, shop for the lowest repair quotes when the car gave out, and adjust the thermostat to keep the summer electric bill from spiking. What she didn't realize was how deeply this pattern was etched into her mindset: money was always tight. Always something to guard, not grow. Something you held on to, not something you could use to build a bigger future.

That belief followed her like a quiet shadow. Through high school. Through college. Even into a career in bookkeeping, where she knew the rules—save, budget, avoid debt—and still couldn't quite believe that money could ever feel safe, let alone abundant.

Taking risks with money? That felt dangerous. Investing in the stock market? That seemed like gambling. Starting her own business? Felt too uncertain. Even spending a little more on things that might truly add value—a better apartment, skills training, or clothes that boosted her confidence at work—seemed frivolous.

"What if I need that money later?" was her go-to line. Her scarcity pattern was evident.

Julie couldn't see what she might gain; she only saw what she could lose. Every time.

What if she invested in mutual funds and the market crashed like it did in 2008? What if she bought a condo and property values dipped? What if she left her safe job to start something of her own, and she couldn't find any clients?

It became second nature—even her coworkers noticed. Here she was, a smart, successful office manager witnessing her clients make savvy financial moves, yet she kept 80 percent of her own money in a low-interest savings account. Julie was watching others build wealth while she was clinging to cash like it was the only lifeline.

It wasn't until her late thirties that something shifted. Slowly. Not due to a sudden "aha" moment, but because of her clients. She began noticing her own scarcity pattern as well as the patterns of others around her, which focused more on abundance. Maria, a schoolteacher earning half of Julie's income, invested regularly and had built a solid portfolio. Kevin, a freelancer with unpredictable paychecks, owned a rental property that generated monthly income.

These weren't reckless people. They were thoughtful, strategic, and willing to take calculated risks.

One day, Julie finally voiced the question that had been nagging at her. "But what if the market crashes?" she asked Maria.

Maria smiled gently. "Then I'll buy more shares while they're low. But Julie... what if it doesn't crash? What if you're so focused on protecting yourself from a loss that never happens, you miss out on twenty years of growth?"

That question lingered, so Julie started doing something she was very comfortable with: crunching numbers. And what she discovered surprised her. If she had invested even a small part of her savings a decade earlier, her net worth would have almost doubled. Playing it safe had quietly cost her thousands of dollars.

So she started making her own investments. Not all at once, just a little every month into something manageable, a diversified fund, even if it still made her a little nervous.

Instead of thinking gains were meant for others, she began asking new questions for herself.

"What if staying stuck costs me more in the long run?" instead of "What if I lose this?"

And that was the turning point. She became aware of her pattern. She stopped evaluating financial choices solely as high-risk or no-risk and began considering the risk of doing nothing at all. Of standing still.

What about childhood caution? Julie still carries some of it, and it serves her well. It makes her a thoughtful investor. She does her homework. She doesn't chase trends, but when that old fear pops up, she has a new perspective: real financial security isn't just about protecting your money; it's about learning how to put it to work.

And more importantly, trust that you are allowed to grow, not just survive. This new pattern represents a form of wealth.

Emily and Julie both realized something powerful: our early experiences with money do leave a deep imprint, but they do not have to define our future. When we start noticing the patterns we have absorbed and their subtle influence on our decisions, we can begin making gentle, intentional changes. This isn't about rejecting where we came from but about moving forward with more awareness and choice. That's what this chapter encourages you to do—start making money decisions that reflect who you are now, not just what you learned back then. Let your money align with your current life and guide you toward the future you desire.

After hearing these stories, imagine how it would feel if your money choices genuinely supported the life you're living, not just the one you think you're supposed to build.

What if spending, saving, investing, and earning all reflected your values, needs, and life seasons?

What if money felt less like a rulebook and more like a tool?

Your financial life doesn't have to look like someone else's. Not your parents'. Not your partner's. Not your advisor's model portfolio. And not even the rigid version you've internalized from years of playing it safe.

Letting your money align with your life means learning to trust your own rhythm. It means releasing the idea that there's a right way to do things, and replacing it with a question: What's right for me, right now?

This is where we begin to move forward with confidence. Not because we have mastered everything but because we are no longer trying to fit our lives into someone else's financial mold.

Recognizing Your Own Money Patterns

Emily and Julie both had moments of recognition; times when they began to recognize the patterns they'd been unconsciously repeating. Emily realized she was chasing windfalls just like her parents had, while Julie understood her caution, though protective, had become restrictive.

But how do you spot your own patterns when you're living inside them?

Your body often knows before your mind does. Notice what happens when you check your bank balance, pay bills, or consider a purchase. Does your chest tighten? Do you hold your breath? Or perhaps you feel a rush of control, relief, or even excitement. These physical responses are signals. They are telling you something about your relationship with money.

Pay close attention to your automatic thoughts as well. When an opportunity arises, what is your first instinct?

I can't afford that.
That's too risky.
I don't deserve this.
Or maybe, *I'll figure it out later.*
I can put it on the card.
I earned this.

These aren't just thoughts. They are scripts you have inherited.

Your patterns also show up in how you handle unexpected situations. When an unexpected expense arises, do you panic or calmly manage your finances to cover it? When you receive a bonus, do you spend it right away or save it? And how do you feel about your choice either way? There is no right answer, but there is your answer, and it reveals something about the money story you carry.

The goal isn't to judge these patterns but simply to observe them. Because once you can recognize them, you can decide whether they still serve your life. Some patterns help you. Others have outlived their usefulness. The key is to develop enough awareness to distinguish between the two. Remember, money isn't a chore—it's a choice.

Recognition is the first step toward making a choice, and that is where your financial story begins to change.

As your money story changes, you get to decide what to keep and what to let go. It's a little like cleaning out a closet: you keep the pieces that fit and feel good, and you let go of what is outdated, no longer brings you joy, or simply feels too tight.

When you shift the way you think about money, you naturally change how you use it. You stop reacting out of habit and begin making intentional choices that reflect who you are now, not just where you came from. Remember, money doesn't control you; it is a tool you can shape, direct, and put to work for the life you want to build.

Money is Simply a Tool

One of the most important mindset shifts we can make is to view money for what it truly is: a tool. That's all it is. It's not a judgment of our worth, a symbol of success (or failure), or a scorecard for how well we are doing (or not doing) in life. Money is simply a means of exchange; it holds no inherent value until we trade it for something else.

We assign meaning to money when we use it—when we exchange it for time, freedom, opportunity, security, or joy. Left untouched, it's just numbers in an account. But when we use it deliberately, it becomes more than that. Not because money itself is inherently powerful, but because our choices in how we use it grant us power.

We don't attach emotional baggage to other tools. No one questions whether they deserve to use a pen, worries about being judged for using scissors, or feels guilty about picking up a fork and knife at dinner. These are simply tools we use without hesitation to accomplish tasks. Money should be no different. However, somewhere along the way, it became emotionally charged, something to validate oneself with, or something to pursue, to hoard, or to regret.

That mindset is what keeps people stuck. Especially women, who have been taught for generations to be cautious, but not confident, with money.

Izzy's calm approach to confronting fear and his practical perspective on money influenced me and began to shift my thinking. Just as he would ask, "What's the worst that can happen?" when facing fear, I started to ask a different type of question about money: What do I want this to help me achieve? That single question transformed my perspective on money—from something I worried about to something I could actually manage.

Cash Isn't Always King

When Julie finally ran the numbers on what her safe strategy had cost her, she realized she wasn't alone. Holding most of her money in cash felt responsible—until she saw how much potential growth she had missed. Turns out, her approach reflects a broader trend. According to BlackRock, women keep about 71 percent of their wealth in cash, compared to 60 percent for men.

But this gap isn't about women being "bad with money." Far from it. Women are often exceptional savers. They're thoughtful, disciplined, and diligent in managing household budgets. What many of us haven't been taught, though, is how to grow the money we have saved. There's a big difference between protecting your money and making it work for you.

The messages many women grow up with are well-meaning but incomplete:

Be careful.

Don't take chances.

Always save for a rainy day.

And while there's nothing wrong with being prudent, girls are often given only half the story. Meanwhile, boys are more likely to hear about building wealth, taking risks, and investing to get ahead. Over time, this creates a gap—not only in knowledge but also in confidence and outcomes. Cash may seem like the safest option, but over time, it quietly loses value, especially when inflation is at play.

Inflation continues to persist in the background, but it can have a significant impact over time. Based on the data from the U.S. Census Bureau, Federal Reserve, and Bureau of Labor Statistics, the cost of housing and everyday goods has outpaced the growth of cash savings, while long-term stock market investments have significantly outperformed both inflation and rising costs.

For context, the median home price in the U.S. was approximately $120,000 in 2000. By 2025, that figure had climbed to over $415,000. That's how inflation and market growth show up in real life, making everyday goals like homeownership significantly more expensive over time.

Now, imagine you had $170,000 in cash in 2000. If you kept it in a standard savings account, its value would have grown slowly—mainly through interest and inflation adjustments—reaching about $315,000 in purchasing power by 2025. That sounds like a lot, but it still wouldn't be enough to afford that median home price, leaving you more than $100,000 short.

But if you had invested that same $170,000 in the U.S. stock market's S&P 500 (which comprises the 500 largest public traded companies) and reinvested the dividends, your money could have grown to over one million dollars by 2025. That's the power of long-term investing: it not only keeps pace with inflation but also allows for real growth.

This trend is not limited to large purchases, such as homes. Everyday items have also experienced significant price increases. For example, the average price of a gallon of milk in 2000 was $2.78, whereas in 2025, it was approximately $4.02. This illustrates how the purchasing power of cash savings has not kept pace with the rising cost of living.

You aren't trying to time the market or chase every hot stock. This example demonstrates how money can grow when it is given the time and space to do so.

The tendency to overlook equity investments is not limited to low- or medium-income households. Even among affluent households, women consistently have less exposure to the public stock market, individual stocks, or mutual funds. Data from the Bank of America Institute shows that women in similar wealth brackets as men have 34 percent less exposure to stocks, often opting for capital preservation instead. This reality, combined with a longer life expectancy—women in the US live on average 5.1 years longer than men—creates a risky mismatch.

UBS modeling clearly highlights this issue: a sixty-five-year-old woman with 50 percent of her portfolio in cash has a 63 percent chance of outliving her savings. In contrast, a more diversified, equity-focused portfolio reduces that probability to 41 percent. While 41 percent is still relatively high and concerning, it serves as yet another reason to implement better controls and plans earlier in life.

Of course, you don't want to take reckless risks, but understand that avoiding risk entirely can be risky in itself. Financial fluidity means making informed, strategic decisions that reflect both your goals and your realities. Cash can provide short-term security, but it should be used as a tool, not a long-term strategy.

Money isn't the goal; it's not the destination. It's merely one of the tools we use to build the life we desire. Once we begin to recognize money patterns and shift our mindset, fear starts to diminish, shame begins to fade, and decisions become clearer.

Risk Isn't Recklessness

Most of us weren't taught how to analyze risk. We were taught to avoid it.

Don't lose what you already have.
Play it safe.
Stick to what is proven.

Especially when it comes to money, women are often encouraged to stay in the lane of safety and stability. Risk, we're told, is something to be approached with caution, if at all.

So, it's no surprise that women are often labeled as risk-averse.

When in reality, many women aren't risk-averse. They're risk-astute, like Liz and Monique, who we will learn about next.

They don't blindly jump in, and they shouldn't.

They want to understand where the risks lie, what's at stake, and how these align with their bigger goals.

That's not hesitation, that's discernment.

Consider Liz, a sales manager who wanted to pursue her master's degree. The conventionally safe choice was to stay in her current job. She had a mortgage, a steady income, and benefits. But when she paused to ask herself, *Is this aligned with where I want to be in five years?* she realized the bigger risk was staying in a role that no longer challenged her.

Liz didn't make this decision impulsively. She researched the program thoroughly, calculated exactly how much she would need to cover expenses during graduate school, and negotiated a part-time consulting arrangement with her employer. She used savings she had been keeping for exactly this kind of opportunity. After completing the program eighteen months later, the combination of her new degree and strategic networking led to a promotion that resulted in a 40 percent salary increase.

That's risk astuteness—thorough evaluation, strategic planning, and actions aligned with long-term goals.

Avoiding risk, or never learning to take calculated ones, can quietly keep you stuck. Stuck in jobs that drain you, relationships you've outgrown, and lives that look fine on the outside but feel empty on the inside.

Staying stuck is a pattern too. It's the pattern of choosing comfort over possibility and familiarity over fulfillment.

Another example is Monique, who had been contributing to her company's 401(k) but kept all her funds in the most conservative money market option (essentially a very low-risk, low-return, cash-like fund) because she felt stocks were too risky. When she calculated that her money was barely keeping pace with inflation, she realized her caution was actually the riskier choice given her thirty-year retirement timeline. She didn't move everything into aggressive growth funds overnight. Instead, she gradually shifted to a balanced portfolio appropriate for her age and goals, accepting short-term volatility in exchange for long-term growth potential.

Being risk-astute is about asking insightful questions before taking action. That isn't a sign of weakness. It's wisdom.

Every meaningful decision involves risk. Starting a business. Pursuing further education. Asking for a raise. Investing in yourself. Saying no to discomfort.

The question isn't, "Is this risky?"

The real question is, "Is this aligned?"

Because *safe* and *right* aren't always the same.

And sometimes, the safer choice is the one that keeps you stuck.

Women are often perceived as risk-averse, or what we've simply called risk-astute, but many are just risk-unpracticed. They weren't invited into conversations where risk was framed as opportunity. They weren't taught that risk can be thoughtful, strategic, and deeply personal.

And here's something else we don't talk about enough: There's risk in staying small, too.

In waiting. In not trusting yourself. In making the smart choice even though it doesn't fit your life anymore.

Letting your money align with your life means reframing risk, not as something to fear but as something to manage.

You get to define your own version of acceptable risk.

You get to decide what's worth stretching for and what's not.

Risk isn't recklessness.

It's simply movement with intention.

And you don't have to get it perfect.

You just must be willing to move.

Rewriting the Rules

This journey of honoring your past while shaping your future unfolds in layers, through daily choices and gradual changes in your relationship with money. It requires both courage and compassion: the courage to choose differently from others' expectations, and compassion for the experiences that shaped those expectations. It's about understanding that the financial patterns you inherited were often born out of love, necessity, or survival, and that choosing differently is not betrayal but growth. All the women featured in this book found their own way to connect their histories with their hopes. They have shown us what it looks like to honor your roots while actively creating your path forward.

Your parents' financial fears may have been completely rational for their circumstances—but they could be completely limiting for yours.

Your family's money rules may have provided crucial stability in the past, but now feel like unnecessary restrictions.

Your early experiences with financial insecurity may have taught you valuable lessons about resilience, as well as unhelpful beliefs about what is possible.

Honoring the past doesn't mean staying trapped by it. It means understanding the lessons it taught you, appreciating the strengths it gave you, and then choosing which parts still serve your life today.

Reflection Questions

What patterns are you noticing in how you spend, save, or invest?

Where are you being thoughtfully strategic? Where might fear be standing in your way?

___

___

___

Have you labeled yourself in the past as risk-averse? How has risk influenced your life in the past?

___

___

___

Like Julie, who keeps a portion of her money in cash, where might your protective strategies be costing you growth or opportunity?

___

___

___

How could resistance to change prevent you from achieving the financial future you desire?

___

___

___

Chapter Seven

Live Financial Fluidity

Between the lessons of the past and the promises of the future, we must remember that life itself is a special occasion worth celebrating.

A friend of mine told me a story I'll never forget. Her family had gathered to celebrate her mother's seventy-fifth birthday. It was a full house, filled with children, grandchildren, and laughter. The kind of moment you want to bottle up and keep forever. She turned to her father, who was an avid wine collector, and suggested they open one of the really nice bottles to add to the celebration. He shook his head and said, "We're saving the good wine for a special occasion."

She thought to herself, *What could be more special than this?*

Within six weeks, her father passed away. The bottle of wine remained unopened.

It's a heartbreaking reminder of how often we postpone joy. We hold back from buying the shoes, wearing the outfit we love, or opening the wine we've been saving. We tell ourselves we're waiting for the right time, a bigger milestone, or the perfect moment. But life is happening right now.

The celebration can be right here, right now, with the people you love, in the milestones you've already reached, in the ordinary moments that become extraordinary when you let them. Buy the shoes. Drink the wine. Light the candle. Stop saving everything good for someday, because someday isn't guaranteed.

I was reminded of this when my mom passed away, and I inherited all her china, along with her mother's. None of it was particularly expensive or fancy. It was just what people did in earlier generations, collecting a full set of dishes for special occasions. After unpacking it, I realized something: No one is going to care about this after I'm gone. It won't be treasured in the way it once was. So why not use it now? Why not eat dinner off the special plates on an ordinary Tuesday night while I can actually enjoy them?

Holding back doesn't make life more meaningful. Living now does. The wine, the china, the little luxuries—we honor them most when we use them, not when we hide them away.

Sometimes our thoughts can convince us to wait, to downplay, or to postpone joy until we've earned it or hit the next milestone. But waiting only robs us of those moments. Choosing to enjoy life now is not reckless; it is a way of refusing to let anything dictate how and when we're allowed to feel joy.

It is for these everyday special occasions that we need financial fluidity. In Chapter 1, we defined financial fluidity as using money to create a life that aligns with your values. It reminds us to live in the present, encourages us to value joy, and enables us to celebrate daily life as a special occasion. It's about making intentional choices rather than reactive ones. And it's about having the resilience to adapt to life's changes, whether that means scaling back, moving forward, or taking a pause.

These choices are part of a flexible framework that serves your actual life. Traditional budgeting often fails because it assumes life is predictable and that everyone's path should look

Live Financial Fluidity

the same. Financial fluidity acknowledges that your twenties differ from your forties, that unexpected opportunities arise, and that sometimes the most responsible choice involves reshaping the mold.

Think of it like learning to drive. At first, you follow every rule precisely—both hands firmly gripping the wheel, making complete stops, and honoring the speed limit. As you gain experience, you learn when to flow with traffic, when to take a different route, and when to make quick judgement calls. You continue to be a safe driver while responding to real conditions rather than following a rigid script.

Financial fluidity in real life means not panicking when plans change but adapting to them. You don't abandon your values because something unexpected occurs; instead, you return to them and let them guide your next step.

Financial fluidity creates a solid foundation that enables you to adapt without breaking. It provides the space to navigate change with clarity rather than shame. It allows you to make decisions based on alignment instead of fear, and to let your values lead, even when life throws you a curveball.

You can save for the future and still tend to what matters now.

You can plan and still pivot effectively.

You can be responsible while remaining flexible.

Fluidity is about choice, presence, and, above all, trust—trust that you don't need a perfect formula, just a clear understanding of what matters most to you and the courage to let your money reflect that.

How to Practice Financial Fluidity in Daily Life

So how do you live financial fluidity?

It starts with noticing when you are acting out of habit instead of intention, or when you follow a pattern simply because it was taught to you, not because it suits your life now.

Unapologetic Wealth

Perhaps you set a strict budget, but then an unexpected opportunity arises—a weekend getaway that energizes you, a class that excites you, or a project that lights you up. The rigid part of you says, *Stick to the plan.* But fluidity encourages you to pause and ask, *Can I adjust to make room for this? Is this worth it?* That's not irresponsibility. That's responsiveness.

Or maybe you feel overwhelmed by the demands of work, caregiving, and daily life. You consider ordering takeout or hiring help, but that familiar voice echoes: *Shouldn't I be able to handle this?* Fluidity allows you to ask a better question: What do I need right now? Sometimes spending is about survival. Sometimes it's about relief. Sometimes it's about honoring your capacity.

Fluidity also appears when you allow yourself to spend on joy. Buying something that makes your life easier or more beautiful doesn't need to be justified by logic or sacrifice. Simply wanting it, truly and honestly, is enough.

And sometimes fluidity means pausing a plan. Perhaps you've been working toward a goal that no longer feels right. You're not quitting; you're realigning. There's strength in knowing when to stay the course and when to pivot.

And when you're sitting across from an advisor or anyone offering financial guidance, fluidity means asking what you need to know. It means trusting your instincts, even if you don't have all the right words yet. You can disagree, even if someone's more experienced. You can take a moment to think. You can ask additional questions. You can say, "This doesn't feel right—yet."

That's what financial fluidity looks like.

Not perfect execution. Not rigid control.

Just steady self-awareness, season after season.

It's a practice built on clarity, intention, and the belief that you're allowed to change your mind as your life evolves.

When Financial Fluidity Gets Complicated

Living with financial fluidity sounds great in theory. It is flexible, intentional, and empowering. But what if life gets messy? When your choices don't land well with those who care, or when a fluid decision ends up being harder than expected?

Women must navigate the tension between planning and flexibility, between honoring their values and adapting to circumstances. Here are real stories of how that looks in practice.

Monique, mentioned in the previous chapter, struggled with fluidity when she shifted from a conservative savings approach to a growth-oriented investment strategy. Her parents, who had experienced multiple recessions and understood the pain of market downturns, didn't hold back.

"You're gambling with your future," her dad said during the family dinner. "We didn't work this hard so you could throw it away on risky stocks."

Oof. The guilt hit her instantly and deeply. These were the people who had taught her everything she knew about managing money. Now, here she was, choosing a path they couldn't support. It felt like a betrayal.

But Monique wasn't chasing crypto or day trading. She understood that, with a long-term perspective, staying in cash was riskier than investing in a diversified portfolio. She had done her homework. What felt like gambling to her parents was actually a thoughtful strategy designed for someone with more than thirty years until retirement.

The solution wasn't to dismiss their concerns or discard her plan. It was to change how she discussed it. Instead of seeking approval, she provided clarity. "I hear you," she'd say, "and I've thought a lot about this." This became her new mantra—respectful yet confident. She stopped trying to persuade them and began standing firm in her decisions.

Sometimes, being financially fluid means making peace with the fact that not everyone will understand your choices. And that's okay.

Janette's perspective was different. She valued experiences, travel, learning, and meaningful connections more than material possessions. So, she used her extra income on trips and retreats that nourished her soul.

But then her car broke down permanently. She faced a tough decision: use her travel fund to buy a reliable car outright or take out a car loan that would strain her monthly budget and limit her flexibility. Neither option felt ideal. A car loan seemed like the kind of financial rigidity she wanted to avoid, but draining the travel fund felt like a sacrifice of the very experiences that brought her happiness and energy.

This is where financial fluidity truly appears—not in choosing the perfect path but in intentionally navigating imperfect realities. Janette chose the car loan. Instead of criticizing herself, she reframed the decision: rather than simply buying a car, she was investing in safety, independence, and peace of mind. Those are valuable priorities as well.

She cut back on her travel but didn't stop completely; instead, she explored creative options like house-sitting gigs and shorter trips. This fluidity aligned with her goals.

Financial fluidity is about knowing what matters most, making space for reality, and staying connected to your values, even when things don't go exactly as planned.

In the previous chapter, we saw Liz's higher education journey conclude on a high note, but what if it hadn't? What if the degree program had fallen flat? What if the job market had slowed down just as she was ready to reenter it? What if the role she'd been hoping for simply didn't materialize?

This is one of the biggest fears people face when they consider stepping away from rigid financial plans: What if I make the wrong choice?

However, here's what financial fluidity reminds us: only a few choices are truly final. Most decisions are simply steps that lead to new information. Even if Liz's time away hadn't led directly to a promotion, it still wouldn't have been a failure—it would have been a learning experience. She would still have gained skills, built connections, and likely uncovered more clarity about what she wanted. That's not insignificant. That's movement.

Sometimes, what feels like a mistake leads to a new and better path. Perhaps that dull degree program introduces you to a professor who then invites you to join a start-up, that turns out to be a perfect fit. Perhaps missing out on the job you wanted pushes you toward consulting, providing the flexibility and freedom you didn't realize you needed. Maybe, just maybe, the whole experience helps you realize that the field of your first choice was never quite right and that clarity saves you from years of frustration.

That's the subtle magic of financial fluidity: it allows for rerouting. What looks like a detour may ultimately prove to be the real path after all.

It is a myth that decisions are final, and this myth can be paralyzing. The point is to make decisions that reflect where you are, what you value, and what you are willing to explore. From there, you adjust. Learn. Recalculate if needed. You are developing new patterns of fluidity.

When we stop treating money as a scoreboard and start seeing it as a tool, our perspective changes. Mistakes aren't proof of failure. They are learning opportunities. And sometimes, those so-called mistakes are what lead you to exactly where you needed to go, even if it's not where you initially thought you were headed.

Let Your Life Lead

Financial fluidity started to make sense to me when I stopped striving for perfection and began being mindful of my money choices. Not just whether they added up, but whether they aligned with my values.

I grew up believing that being careful with money was of prime importance. And for a long time, this belief served me well. It pushed me to save. It kept me out of debt. But it also kept me small. I hesitated to invest in things that mattered to me. I double-checked every decision, not just with my calculator but also with my sense of self-worth.

Financial fluidity enables you to shift from reacting to choosing.

Financial fluidity allows you to keep what serves you and release what doesn't. To say, "Thank you for keeping us safe," to the old patterns while choosing new ones that fit your current reality.

This is how you reshape the future. You don't have to reject where you came from, but you can consciously choose where you are going.

Financial fluidity means you grant yourself the grace to adapt without shame. You stop chasing perfection and start building adaptability that reflects your values, your capacity, and your season of life.

There will still be calendars. Plans. Responsibilities.

But now, they follow *your* life. Not the other way around.

Now you know what it looks like to step into financial leadership with quiet consistency and self-awareness. Now you have begun to ask the right questions:

What do I want my money to make possible?

What kind of life am I actually creating?

How can my financial choices reflect who I'm becoming, not just who I've been?

And perhaps most importantly: how can I honor the wisdom of my past while claiming the possibilities of my future?

As you start to answer those questions, you are no longer following someone else's financial blueprint. You're creating your own.

Reflection Questions

Acknowledging your past, which specific beliefs or behaviors regarding money feel outdated for your current life?

_____

_____

_____

Consider a recent situation where you felt trapped by rigid financial rules or expectations. How might you have approached it differently with greater flexibility and intention?

_____

_____

_____

Can you think of a friend who demonstrated financial fluidity in the face of challenges? What lessons can you draw from their example?

_____

_____

_____

What would financial fluidity look like in your daily life?

_____

_____

_____

What would it feel like to let your life lead your money decisions?

_____

_____

_____

What would you like to carry forward, and what are you ready to evolve?

_____

_____

_____

Chapter Eight

Redefine Wealth

I remember hearing the song "Cat's in the Cradle" by Harry Chapin when I was growing up. Even as a child, it made me feel uneasy, like there was a loss I couldn't quite identify—if I wasn't careful, I could lose something important in my own life as well.

As I grew older, I came to understand it more deeply.

It's a story about a father who is too busy to spend time with his son. Always working, always focused on the future. Later, when there's more time. Later, when things slow down. Later, when the money is right. But later never really comes. And by the time the son grows up, he is living out the same pattern—always busy, always chasing something just out of reach.

It's a song about choices. About what we prioritize. Yes, on the surface, it is about money. But more than that, it is about what gets lost when we let money drive our decisions.

I'm not suggesting we throw caution to the wind or pretend money doesn't matter. We all know the saying, "Money can't buy happiness," and while that is true, money can buy time, options, security, and ease—and those things matter.

What if we could loosen our grip just enough to regain control from the fear or pressure we associate with money? What if we could redefine wealth on our own terms—terms that reflect what truly matters?

We can.

We can redefine wealth to reflect not just what is earned and accumulated, but also what is felt and how we really want to live. We can create financial lives that promote connection, presence, and choice. And we can pass down values rooted in alignment.

This chapter is an invitation to look at wealth differently.

Not only for what you accumulate but also for what you experience.

And perhaps, to realize, you might already be building it.

Real Wealth

When most people hear the word wealth, they think of accumulation: a specific income, a particular retirement account balance, and a certain lifestyle. Wealth, in this traditional sense, is tied to visible markers of success such as homes, salaries, cars, and vacations. And for many women, especially those raised to be practical and cautious with money, it is also connected to the idea of enoughness—but only once it has been earned, saved, and proven.

These definitions are everywhere. But they are narrow. They are myopic. And for many, they are quietly exhausting.

What traditional measures of wealth often overlook are your time, your freedom, your health, and your peace of mind. It's about how much space you have in your day to rest, create, care for others, or take care of yourself. The Dalai Lama summed up our backward pursuit of value in one sharp observation: We trade health for wealth, then spend that wealth trying to buy our health back. This serves as a reminder to prioritize what truly matters and to ensure it lasts.

Real wealth might be the ability to leave work early to attend your child's school event, or to take a break to go to a yoga class, or to simply close your eyes for fifteen minutes in the middle of the day.

It might be the freedom to say no to a toxic client or friend, or to accept a job that pays less but allows you to set your own hours.

It might mean cooking a meal without rushing or spending an entire afternoon doing absolutely nothing without feeling guilty. And by doing these things, we are not lowering our standards. We are broadening our definition.

When wealth is defined by energy, ease, and alignment—not just income or status—it becomes more personal and authentic.

Perhaps success is not something you are meant to prove; rather, it is something you are meant to live.

Imagine not having to rack up the monetary possessions—the bigger house, the nicer car, the constant upgrades—just to feel like you've made it. Imagine measuring success by your ability to find a new calm amid chaos and alignment in everyday life.

A New Kind of Rich

Rachel and her husband had one son, and after years of trying unsuccessfully for a second child, she quietly let go of hope. Life moved on, and they adjusted to being a family of three. Then, nearly nine years after their first child, Rachel unexpectedly found herself pregnant.

Their second child was born into a home filled with gratitude and relief, but the early years were challenging. Medical issues, sleepless nights, and uncertain outcomes became part of the daily routine. As her daughter began to stabilize and thrive, Rachel started reflecting on how she wanted to spend her time, how she earned money, and what kind of presence she wanted to have in her children's lives.

She realized that the true gift she was seeking wouldn't come from financial security alone but from flexibility. So, she started small: a home-based business assisting people with planning and organizing events. It gave her control. She could set her own schedule, choose her clients, and gradually teach herself new skills like graphic design, marketing, and content strategy, so she could offer more services and increase her earnings.

Eventually, the business grew to the point where she enlisted help from family members. She created not only a job but also a path for growth and fulfillment. Most importantly, she built a life that enabled her to leave work early to attend a school performance, sit beside her daughter at a doctor's appointment, or simply enjoy a quiet afternoon without having to explain herself to a boss.

Rachel continues to work hard. She thinks about money, plans for the future, and makes smart decisions. However, her definition of wealth isn't about a salary raise or chasing a number. It's about living a life that reflects what matters most.

Time. Autonomy. Presence. That's her version of rich. And she's building it intentionally.

Rethinking Enough

If you've ever thought, *I'll feel better once I*...get my to-do list under control, lose those ten pounds, or land that next raise—you're not alone. We are often taught that peace, confidence, or satisfaction exists just beyond the next achievement. That enough is close but still at least one accomplishment away.

The finish line keeps moving. How much is enough? When do you rest and smell the metaphorical roses? When do you stop second-guessing yourself? Most of us don't know because we have never been taught to define these moments for ourselves.

We're often advised to manage our money wisely: save for the future, prepare for emergencies, and live within our means. However, these guidelines are usually vague, and, more importantly, they lack emotional context. What if you are doing fine financially but still don't feel settled? What if no amount of income can quiet the feeling that you should be doing more?

Well, *enough* is about being honest with yourself about what you need to feel secure and aligned. Numbers can help, but it takes more than just number crunching.

Start by honestly defining what financial security means to you. Not what others have told you it should mean, but what would genuinely help you sleep better at night.

What do you fear might happen if you have less? Are these fears based on your actual experience, or are they stories you've inherited from your family, culture, or past versions of yourself that may no longer serve you?

Think back to times when you felt most at peace with your financial situation. What was different about those moments? Often, it wasn't the amount of money but the clarity about what truly mattered and the confidence in your own ability to handle whatever came next.

Enough will shift as your life changes. It looks different at twenty-five with no dependents than at forty with kids or aging parents. That's normal and healthy. But if your idea of 'enough' changes every time you get close to reaching it, you risk confusing progress with failure and never finding true alignment.

Virginia realized she had been chasing a moving target for years. Initially, she aimed to save ten thousand dollars for emergencies. Once she achieved that, she decided to increase her goal to twenty thousand. After reaching that, she then determined she needed to save six months' worth of expenses instead of three. Each time she hit a goal, instead of feeling proud or relieved, she immediately set a new, higher one.

She didn't realize that her behavior was an inherited pattern until she asked herself a different question: What am I afraid of? Then the pattern began to shift. The answer wasn't about money; it was about feeling out of control. Once she recognized this, she was able to address the real issue. She kept a reasonable emergency fund and focused her energy on developing skills and fostering relationships that provided her with a genuine sense of security. From there, instead of primarily keeping her money in cash, she could start exploring other investment avenues that might lead to more profitable outcomes.

Enough became a moving target, not because she was chasing more, but because she was waiting for someone or something to tell her it was finally okay to choose herself without guilt.

No one else is going to grant you that permission. You have to give it to yourself.

I believe this idea is so important that you need to hear it again. *You* have the power to grant yourself permission to choose when is enough. It may be enough for an hour, a day, a year, or longer, but you get to decide.

Enough might be knowing you can cover an unexpected bill without borrowing. It might be the ability to choose rest when you're tired, not just when everything is done. It might mean working less, earning less, and doing more of what makes your life feel aligned with who you are.

Your decisions are not set in stone; they can change with your values, responsibilities, and the seasons of your life. Once you define success for yourself, it becomes much easier to stop chasing someone else's version of it and start living your own.

Creating Culture

Lucey is a brilliant scientist and the founder of a women's health company dedicated to developing a treatment for endometriosis, a field that has long lacked research, funding, and attention. She leads a small, committed team of ten employees who are passionate about creating solutions that could change lives. However, the potential for great impact comes with significant pressure. Every stage of their work requires funding: from preclinical trials and manufacturing to regulatory strategy. And that funding depends on achieving specific milestones that bring them closer to Food and Drug Administration (FDA) approval.

Milestones, in theory, should represent moments of progress. But for Lucey, they've become checkpoints on a treadmill that never stops.

Every twelve to eighteen months, the team reaches a major milestone, an achievement that demands grit, late-night vigor, and creative problem-solving. Before even thinking of celebration, they jump back into fundraising. Long hours. Pitch decks. Meetings with investors. Explaining, defending, convincing.

Fundraising is hard. Growing a health-tech company as a woman in a male-dominated industry is even harder.

Lucey doesn't stop to celebrate, not because she isn't proud but because the next challenge is already looming. The next finish line appears before the previous one is barely acknowledged. She tells herself she'll take a breath once they reach FDA approval, once the product launches, once they are truly changing lives. But even she is beginning to wonder whether that moment will ever feel like enough.

This pattern is costing her more than she initially realized. She is missing dinners with her partner, who has started eating alone most nights. The creative problem-solving that once energized her now feels mechanical. She is making decisions out of exhaustion rather than insight. Her body is sending signals she is ignoring: tension headaches, disrupted sleep, and a persistent feeling of falling behind, even when things are going well.

Her team is feeling it too. Two of her top researchers have mentioned being "curious about other opportunities." Meetings that once buzzed with excitement now seem solely focused on the endless tasks that await. The shared sense of purpose that originally united them is being overshadowed by a constant sense of urgency.

Lucey knows something needs to change, but she is caught in a familiar trap. *If I slow down, we might lose momentum*, she tells herself. *I can't ask people to celebrate when there's still so much at stake*. She fears that taking a moment to acknowledge progress might be perceived as her not being driven enough or serious enough about the timeline.

Lucey is starting to realize that her mission's sustainability depends on her ability to continuously redefine what success means.

The wealth she's truly creating isn't just a successful company; it's a sustainable way to make meaningful change. And if she or her team burns out while chasing the ultimate goal, they may never achieve it.

Imagine if things shifted just slightly.

Imagine if, after each milestone, there was a pause. Not a long vacation or an expensive celebration, but a moment to acknowledge how far the team has come. A team lunch where people could share what they're proud of. An afternoon when Lucey could remind everyone, including herself, why this work matters and how much they have already accomplished.

A simple change like this wouldn't slow the momentum; it might actually sustain it. When people feel recognized and appreciated for their contributions, they don't just work harder; they work smarter. They stay longer. They bring more creativity and resilience to future challenges.

Culture would shift. Energy would reset. The team wouldn't just endure the grind—they'd feel proud, energized, and ready for the next phase. And Lucey might discover that the wealth she's building includes more than just impact and income—it also includes a deep satisfaction derived from leading with respect for both the mission and the people who make it possible.

This reframe neither diminishes the urgency of the work nor the importance of the goal. Instead, it acknowledges that sustainable success, the kind that leads to lasting change, requires a different kind of wealth. One that encompasses presence, acknowledgment, and the wisdom to understand that *how* you build something is just as important as *what* you build. We can recognize this as cultural wealth: the richness of being part of environments where people feel respected, appreciated, and safe to thrive.

Sometimes, the best strategic move is to pause and say, "Look what we have accomplished. Let's honor that before we keep going."

The Many Forms of Wealth

When we expand our definition of wealth beyond bank accounts and stock portfolios, we begin to notice other kinds of riches that have been hiding in plain sight. These forms of wealth usually don't show up on spreadsheets, but they shape the quality of our lives in lasting ways. They're built quietly through small decisions that may not seem flashy but add up to something deeply meaningful.

Relationship Wealth

When Sue moved across the country for a new job, she felt excited and proud. The salary bump was significant, the title a promotion, and the opportunities for growth abundant. It felt like a natural next step. But she hadn't fully anticipated the loneliness that came with leaving her long-standing community. The happy hours and weekend brunches with college friends were suddenly replaced by solo evenings and a calendar filled only with work.

At first, she filled the void by working longer hours at the office. But one night, sitting alone in her apartment after a long week, she realized: no job title could make up for a lack of connection.

So, she began rebuilding, slowly and intentionally. She joined a local book club because she missed the feeling of shared conversation. She volunteered at an animal shelter once a week. She said yes to a coworker's invitation for a hike, even though she didn't love early mornings.

Over time, these small steps added up. When her father had a medical emergency and she needed to fly home on short notice, three different people stepped in—offering to feed her cat, drive her to the airport, and watch over her house while she was away. That moment made it real: Sue wasn't just surviving in a new city—she had built a support system. You can't measure that kind of wealth in dollars, but it matters. Deeply. It's the comfort of knowing you're not navigating life alone.

Time Wealth

Derek used to believe that a packed calendar was a sign of success. As a high-performing consultant, he said yes to everything: early meetings, weekend calls, and red-eye flights. His phone was always in hand, his inbox never cleared, and his evenings blurred into late-night work sessions.

But one evening, while scrolling through emails at the dinner table, his eight-year-old daughter asked, "Why do you always look at your phone more than at me?" That one sentence hit him harder than any client deadline ever had.

He began reevaluating his priorities. Gradually, he began saying no to projects that didn't align with his core values—even the lucrative ones. He carved out pockets of his day that were truly off-limits to work: morning walks, family dinners, and quiet reading at night. Although he took on fewer clients, he was more deeply engaged with those he chose.

His income dropped slightly at first, but the time he gained was priceless. He was there for his daughter's soccer games. He laughed more. Slept better. Felt more like himself. Time wealth wasn't about doing less; it was about doing what mattered, with more presence and less stress.

Health Wealth

Jennifer had always been someone who could power through anything. Five hours of sleep? No problem. Lunch at her desk? Typical. She thrived on to-do lists and wore her burnout like a badge of honor. Her friends joked that she ran on coffee and grit—and in many ways, she actually did.

But during a routine physical, her doctor didn't find her lifestyle amusing. Instead, he said, "Your body is showing signs of chronic stress. This pace is unsustainable." That word—*unsustainable*—echoed in her mind for days.

Jennifer realized she had been borrowing from her health to fund everything else. And now, the bill was coming due.

So, she made some changes. Not overnight, but gradually. She began going to bed earlier, even if her inbox wasn't cleared. She scheduled time for movement—yoga, walks, the occasional dance class—just as she would for a client meeting. She started eating meals at an actual table, without any screens.

The results weren't just physical. With more energy and mental clarity, Jennifer's work improved significantly. Her relationships deepened. She no longer dragged herself through life—she was actively participating. Health wealth became the foundation supporting everything else she wanted to do.

Creative Wealth

Lisa had checked all the boxes. She had a stable job in accounting, a solid retirement plan, and a cozy condo. From the outside, everything seemed perfect. But inside, she felt a dull ache she couldn't quite name. She missed something she couldn't put her finger on.

Then, one Saturday, on a whim, she signed up for a pottery class. Just two hours. Just for fun. And something clicked. Her hands in the clay, the feel of creating something imperfect and real, ignited a part of her she hadn't touched in years.

She kept going. Pottery led to sketching, and sketching into small design projects for friends. Her evenings began to include color and shape, not just spreadsheets and balance sheets. She didn't quit her job—she still appreciated the stability. She didn't have to. She started teaching beginner pottery classes on weekends. The pay wasn't the point; the creative wealth was undeniable.

Lisa felt more alive, more like she was thriving, and more like herself. Creative wealth wasn't about becoming an artist; it was about reclaiming a part of her identity she had buried beneath practicality. It also gave her a new lens to see her whole life through.

Knowledge Wealth

When Marcus was laid off at forty-five, he felt like the industry had left him behind. Digital marketing had exploded, and he worried his years of experience wouldn't count in a world that prized new tech over old-school strategy.

But instead of retreating, he decided to reinvest in himself. He enrolled in online courses to catch up on the latest technologies. He began learning about new trends, watching webinars, and talking to people half his age to understand what was changing.

And something unexpected happened: he began to realize that his strong foundation in traditional marketing gave him a unique perspective. He wasn't behind—he was layered. He combined his old-school knowledge with new-tech learning and started consulting. His clients valued his balanced approach. His business grew.

Marcus now earns more than he did in his corporate role. But more than that, he feels confident. Resilient. Adaptable. That's knowledge wealth—the kind that grows and builds as you do.

The Compound Effect

These kinds of wealth don't live in silos. They nurture each other. Sue's relationships gave her more than support; they strengthened her mental and emotional health.

Derek's time freedom created space for learning and purpose, deepening both his knowledge and his relationships.

Jennifer's focus on her health gave her the energy to reconnect with her creative interests and show up more fully in every part of her life.

Lisa's creative outlet boosted her confidence, enabling her to negotiate greater flexibility in her work schedule.

Marcus's investment in learning reignited a sense of purpose that influenced everything from how he used his time to how he engaged with others.

And the magic is that this non-monetary wealth doesn't diminish when you share it—it expands. When you invest in relationships, you don't just receive support; you also invite others to rely on you. When you prioritize your well-being, you model a different way of living. When you make space for creative or meaningful pursuits, you often inspire others to do the same.

This is the kind of energy that not only nourishes you but also attracts more of the same. The more aligned you are with your values, the more likely you are to connect with people who share them.

This wealth grows through presence, connection, and intention—not through accumulation. And you may already be building it, one quiet choice at a time.

When Wealth Becomes Yours to Define

We have seen that intentionally choosing a different kind of richness, often accepting some financial trade-offs, can provide much more value in return. It's about building lives that truly reflect what matters instead of chasing material success.

This is what happens when you define wealth for yourself. You begin to see abundance in places where you once noticed only dull moments. You realize that the security of deep relationships, the freedom that comes with control over your time, the energy gained from caring for your health, the fulfillment of creative expression, and the confidence built through continuous learning are all valuable forms of wealth that deserve recognition and protection.

Success is something you live, not something you prove.

When you embrace this truth, your choices begin to shift. You might still care about financial security, but you no longer sacrifice your health, relationships, or values to achieve it. You might still set ambitious goals, but you also celebrate progress and incorporate sustainability into your pursuit. You might still want to achieve and contribute, but you do so from a place of alignment rather than anxiety.

This shift isn't about perfection; it's about awareness. It is about recognizing that the narrow definition of wealth you may have inherited doesn't have to define your life. It's about giving yourself permission to value what you *truly* value, not what you think you should value.

The invitation is simple: look at your life through a wider lens. Notice the wealth that's already there. Recognize the forms of richness you've been creating, perhaps without realizing it. Then, make small, daily choices that honor and expand the definition of wealth that feels true to you.

When you define wealth for yourself, you may realize you are already richer than you thought. From this awareness, you can create something more aligned, more sustainable, and more meaningful.

Reflection Questions

What are you currently measuring your success against? Is it your own definition or someone else's?

_____

_____

_____

Which part of your life already reflects your values?

_____

_____

_____

Where could your financial choices better support the life you want to live?

_____

_____

_____

What would it feel like to stop chasing the next milestone and start living with a sense of enough right now? What would change?

_____

_____

_____

Unapologetic Wealth

If money wasn't the objective and you stopped focusing on what wealth should look like, how would you want it to feel?

_____

_____

_____

Chapter Nine

Use Money Intentionally

So far, we have developed the concept that money isn't the enemy, the goal, or the finish line. It's simply a tool. But now it's time to take this idea further.

The real power comes when you start using money intentio*nally* —not just to cover the basics, but to *build* your life. Not reactively, not by default, but with purpose.

There is no universal rulebook. What is smart for one person might feel limiting to another. The only strategy that matters is the one that aligns with your values, your current season, and your vision. This might mean paying off debt, saving more for the future, or it could also mean taking a sabbatical, supporting a friend, hiring a cleaning service, or investing in something you believe in. All that counts.

Sometimes money is a tool for building, which could mean starting a business, getting more education, or buying a home. Other times, it's used for healing, like paying for therapy, taking a class, or giving yourself time to breathe. Money can bring joy, peace, stability, and momentum. It can also help you support others or care for yourself.

There is no single right way, and you don't have to do anything just to look impressive or strategic on paper. What truly matters is whether it fits your life. Remember, there is no set timeline. Some seasons may feel quick and full of momentum, while others take longer to unfold. That's nothing to feel bad about. Growth, healing, and progress all happen on their own schedules.

You might be going through a season where you're building something big or one where you're simply holding things together. Perhaps you're shifting from growth to rest or from survival to dreaming again. Each of these phases calls for a financial approach that respects your current state, not one that shames you for wanting to be there.

Your goals will evolve. Your values will sharpen. What once made sense might no longer fit, and that's not failure. That's progress.

You aren't trying to use money the right way. You want to use it in a way that's right for you. That kind of alignment is powerful. It puts you in the driver's seat—where your money supports your life, not the other way around.

Perhaps you share my perspective and like the idea of doing good while doing well. The idea is that your money can help you achieve your financial goals *and* make a difference. This is more than just something that sounds nice. Increasingly more people, particularly women, are exploring this approach through values-based investing.

You don't have to choose between supporting causes you care about and building your own financial future. You can invest in companies that are addressing real issues, like access to clean water, education, or health care, while still seeking financial returns. Too often, people believe this is only possible by donating to charity—but in reality, you can do it by investing with intention.

Use Money Intentionally

In my book *Do Good While Doing Well*, I explain how angel investing became that bridge for me. I discovered I could support innovative start-ups solving problems I care about, often led by underrepresented founders such as women and people of color, and still have the potential to earn financial returns. Many believe that being among the ultra-rich or being invited to specific investments is the only way to participate. But that is a myth. We can invest our money in ways that reflect our values. This may involve making conscious decisions about where to shop, bank, or dine, all to support local businesses. And you can also invest in companies fighting climate change, improving access to education, or promoting health equity for as little as fifty dollars. (For more information, visit my website at www.marciadawood.com)

This type of investing doesn't have to feel overwhelming. You can start small, ask questions, and learn as you go. Participation is key. When you use your money to support people, ideas, or innovations that align with your vision, you feel more connected to the outcome. That connection strengthens both your purpose and your confidence. That is the true power of intentional investing.

Spending, Saving, and Investing Are All Valid

One of the biggest shifts we need to make is to let go of the judgment we attach to how we use money. Somewhere along the way, spending came to be seen as bad, saving as good, and investing as intimidating. But they all have their place and serve different purposes at different times.

Spending aligns deeply when it reflects your values. Spending on things that reflect your values and satisfy your needs is perfectly valid: taking a trip with your family, hiring help so you can rest, or buying tools to make daily life easier. These are not wasteful. They are intentional. You can use money as a resource to create experiences, comfort, or happiness.

Saving gives you space—space to pause, prepare for a change, or handle the unexpected. However, hoarding money because you feel unworthy, afraid to enjoy what you've earned, or saving out of fear can quietly reinforce a mindset of scarcity. Saving with purpose allows you to make decisions with greater freedom and less panic.

For many women, investing is a topic often avoided because we have been told we don't know enough to do it well. That stops here. You don't need to become an expert overnight, nor do you have to take huge risks. Investing is about making your money work for you over time. It's about planting seeds, not gambling.

An often overlooked truth is that women make exceptional investors due to the unique traits they bring to the table.

Patience.

A steady hand during downturns.

A long-term vision.

A cautious restraint regarding a hot tip or a risky idea that a friend brags about.

These qualities not only protect women from impulsive decisions, but they also often create stronger results. According to Fidelity, women investors earn better returns and experience fewer losses.[ix]

Women consistently demonstrate strong financial instincts across many areas, from investing to entrepreneurship. According to Forbes, a ten-year study by First Round Capital found that companies with at least one female founder outperformed those with all-male founding teams by 63 percent in terms of value created for investors. When women step into the investing space, the data shows they possess more than enough skill to thrive.

And investing is not limited to stocks or retirement accounts. It could also mean starting your own business, buying a rental property, funding a creative project, or supporting someone else's venture. It can even involve investing in yourself through education, therapy, coaching, or volunteering for a cause you care about. Using money wisely doesn't mean managing it the same way all the time. You are allowed to have seasons of spending, saving, investing, and shifting between these approaches as your life evolves.

Investing Can Be Accessible

For too long, investing has been wrapped in unnecessary complexity. It has been considered practicable only for experts, the ultra-wealthy, or finance graduates. But investing is simply the act of making your money work for your future, and it is far more accessible than many people have been led to believe.

You don't need to know everything. You just need enough knowledge to get started and remain open to learning as you progress. This might mean investing in a simple index fund through your retirement account, contributing to a crowdfunding campaign for a start-up you believe in, or exploring opportunities in real estate, art, or small businesses. There is no single right way to begin.

And most people don't hear enough about women being naturally strong investors. Women tend to be thoughtful, research-driven, patient, and less likely to jump at the next get-rich-quick idea, qualities that lead to better long-term outcomes.

What matters most is that you begin. Because waiting until you feel 100 percent confident or fully prepared only leads to endless delays, during which your money remains idle and may even lose value instead of growing. Worse, you reinforce the outdated belief that you're not capable enough to take control.

One of the biggest mindset shifts is realizing that investing isn't reckless—it's responsible. Investing is not about chasing huge returns. It is about building a foundation for future freedom. Every dollar you invest in your future is a reinforcement of your agency and signifies that your dreams are worth planning for.

Yes, ask questions. Yes, seek guidance. But don't give up on investing just because someone once made you feel small in a meeting, or you received a packet of paperwork that made no sense. Those moments are not proof that you're bad with money. They're proof that the system hasn't been designed to include you.

By the time Ginger turned fifty, she felt the weight of a life that no longer fit her. Her work no longer inspired her, her marriage felt hollow, and the town where she had lived for decades seemed to shrink each year. Still, she waited, telling herself that if she kept going, eventually something would change. But nothing shifted on its own. Years passed, and she began to believe the window had closed—that she had run out of time. By holding back, she missed out on opportunities to grow her career, build wealth, and create the stability she longed for in retirement. This is the quiet cost of waiting: the slow erosion of both possibility and security. Yet the truth is, it is never really too late.

Invest anyway. Learn anyway. You're not too late, and you're not behind.

Change at sixty may not look like change at thirty, but it is still possible, still worthwhile, and still within reach.

Nora was in her mid-forties when she realized she had been avoiding her financial future. She had spent years focusing on her career in nonprofit leadership and raising two children, but when a friend asked if she was contributing to her 403(b) retirement plan, she realized she didn't even know how it worked.

"I just assumed someone else was managing it," she told me. "It felt like something I wasn't smart enough to handle."

She realized she needed to make some changes. A few weeks later, she scheduled a meeting with HR, asked about her retirement options, and then went home and started reading articles and listening to relevant podcasts. Although she didn't understand everything, she understood enough to open her account, choose a fund to invest in, and start contributing.

Since then, Nora has accomplished even more. She opened a brokerage account, invested in a women-led startup through a platform recommended by her friend, and even joined a local investing club with several other women from her community.

"I used to think investing was about trying to beat the stock market," she said. "Now, I know it's about building options for my future self."

Nora didn't become a financial expert overnight. She didn't have to. She simply took one step after another, and her confidence grew.

What would Ginger's life have looked like if she had started at fifty when she realized it could be different? What if she had not waited?

The Stock Market and Beyond

When thinking about investing, some people imagine a broker in a suit shouting on a trading floor, just like in the movies. The U.S. public stock market is frequently portrayed as a high-stakes game of rapid moves and quick wins, but that's not how most successful investors approach it. The stock market can be a place to steadily grow wealth over time. Yes, prices fluctuate, sometimes dramatically, but these daily swings don't have to drive your life. Stock market investors who obsess over every dip or spike live with constant anxiety. What matters most is having a clear strategy, staying consistent, and remembering that the long-term trend has historically favored patience over panic.

In addition to the stock market, there are many ways to invest; some you may have heard of before, and others maybe not. If you are wondering, *don't each of these come with a new learning curve?* Don't worry. You don't need to learn about all of them at once. Awareness is key. Knowing that you have options and understanding them are important steps in your decision-making process. Here are some examples.

Peer-to-peer lending enables you to directly borrow from and lend to individuals or small businesses through platforms that connect people. Instead of banks capturing all the profit through interest, you can earn returns while helping someone start a business or pay off debt. Although it carries some risk, peer-to-peer lending is often more transparent and personal than traditional investing.

Real estate investment trusts (REITs) allow you to invest in property without becoming a landlord. You can purchase shares in companies that own apartment buildings, office spaces, or shopping centers, and earn returns from rent income and property appreciation without the responsibilities of owning or maintenance.

Commodities include precious metals like gold and silver, agricultural products such as wheat and coffee, and energy sources like oil. You can invest in commodities through exchange-traded funds (ETFs) that track their prices, without the need to store physical gold bars in your closet or worry about where to keep barrels of oil. Commodity prices often move independently of stock markets and can be influenced by factors ranging from weather patterns to global politics.

Crowdfunding platforms allow you to invest in start-ups, real estate projects, or creative ventures alongside other investors. Whether you are backing a tech company through equity crowdfunding, funding a documentary film, or investing in a new apartment complex, sometimes starting with just a few hundred dollars, you now have opportunities that were once only available to wealthy investors.

Cryptocurrency is often described as everything from digital gold to the future of finance to high-stakes speculation. It is a relatively new form of investment that has captured widespread attention. While Bitcoin and Ethereum are the most well-known, there are thousands of digital currencies, each with its own purpose, level of adoption, and risk. The crypto market is highly volatile, with prices that can rise or fall sharply in short periods, so it is wise to invest only what you can afford to lose. Like any emerging technology, it requires research, awareness, and a tolerance for unpredictability.

Art and collectibles can appreciate in value over time, ranging from original paintings and vintage items to rare books. While

Use Money Intentionally

this requires thorough research and involves unique risks, it allows you to invest in things you are passionate about, genuinely enjoy, and understand. Your investment can literally hang on your wall or sit on your shelf while potentially increasing in value.

Angel and venture capital investing involves providing early-stage funding to start-up companies, often in exchange for equity. Through online platforms, local investor groups, or venture capital firms, you can support entrepreneurs whose missions align with your values, whether they are women-led businesses, sustainable technology, or solutions to problems you care about.

Community investing involves directing your money into local businesses, community development financial institutions, or social impact funds. This approach allows your money to grow while supporting causes you care about, such as affordable housing, small business growth, and environmental sustainability.

Skills and education, of course, are among the highest-return investments you can make. A certification program, a course that teaches you a new skill, or a conference that expands your network should not be considered expenses. Instead, they are investments in your earning potential and career trajectory.

You do not need to become an expert in every type of investment. Simply understand that you have options beyond the stock market, options that can align with your values, your comfort level, and your vision for the impact your money supports in the world.

And yes, you might also invest in individual stocks, ETFs, or index funds—not because you want to be a stock trader, but because you want your money to grow quietly in the background while you focus on your life.

Start with what you're curious about. Don't worry if it feels intimidating at first. That's normal. You are developing a skill set and mindset that were never shown or taught to many women. You're catching up, and you're also moving forward.

Ask questions. Be intentional. Let your money work with you—not against you, not in secret, and not in silence.

Money as a Resource, Not Just Protection

Many of us were taught to view money as a shield, something that keeps us safe. It pays the bills, covers emergencies, and is there for a rainy day. Yes, money can certainly provide protection, but that's only part of the story.

Money can also serve as a resource to help you create, connect, and contribute. It's not just meant to prevent bad things from happening. It also helps good things grow.

Think of money as a bridge.

It can bridge the gap between burnout and rest, isolation and support, survival and thriving. When you view money only as a defense, you overlook its potential as a fuel for your growth.

Interestingly, most of us are wired to protect what we have more than to reach for what we don't. We are more motivated to avoid losing money than to use it to improve our lives. This isn't a personal flaw; it's a psychological bias called "loss aversion," and it has a powerful grip on how we think about money and make decisions.

Psychologists Daniel Kahneman and Amos Tversky discovered that the pain of losing money is approximately twice as intense as the pleasure of gaining the same amount. In other words, losing one hundred dollars hurts far more than gaining one hundred dollars feels good. This imbalance explains why people, even those who are smart and calculated, often avoid financial risks. It's not just about fear; it's about how our brains process loss as emotionally more significant than gain.

In one of their classic studies, participants were offered a fifty-fifty chance to win or lose one hundred dollars. Rationally, it was a fair gamble. But most people rejected it outright. They were not neutral—they were actively averse. On average, people required the potential gain to be about twice the potential loss before they would even consider accepting the gamble.

This instinct isn't just theoretical; it appears everywhere. Investors hold onto losing stocks, hoping they'll bounce back.

Use Money Intentionally

Homeowners refuse to sell at a loss, even when doing so would be the smartest decision. People remain in jobs, relationships, or routines that no longer benefit them because they fear losing the security they already have. And marketers understand this well; they craft messages focused on what you might lose rather than what you could gain, as loss aversion drives our actions.

Imagine someone finds a one-hundred-dollar bill on the street. Maybe they smile, maybe they treat themselves. But now imagine that same person realizes they've just lost one hundred dollars. Their stomach drops. They panic. They retrace every step. The emotional weight is completely different. Same amount of money, two very different reactions.

This is the effect of loss aversion—it distorts our judgment, not because we're irrational but because we're human. And if we view money only as something to protect, we're more likely to remain stuck in safe, familiar patterns, even when better options are available.[x]

Recognizing how loss aversion influences your choices empowers you to pause, reset, and make decisions based on your current values rather than past fears.[xi]

Jessica was a single mother of two who always played it safe with her finances. She saved diligently, avoided risks, and rarely spent money on herself. After a difficult divorce, her mindset was understandably focused on protection. She had worked hard to build a modest safety net and didn't want to risk losing it.

But after a few years, she felt stuck. "I wasn't struggling, but I wasn't growing either," she told me. "I realized I had built a life that was financially secure, but emotionally and creatively starved."

That's when Jessica did something that felt radical for her: she used some of her savings to enroll in a professional training program in interior design, a field she had always been curious about. It wasn't cheap nor was it necessary, but it was deeply aligned with who she was becoming.

From that point, things changed. Jessica began freelancing part-time, and her confidence grew. She was able to say yes to creative projects *while* staying present with her kids. The money she spent wasn't wasted. It was an investment in herself, her future, and her well-being.

The way you use money affects those around you and shapes the world you want to create. When you start viewing money as a means to connect and make a difference, not just a way to ensure security, you unlock some of its most powerful potential.

Think about the last time you used money to connect with someone. Maybe you paid for dinner for a friend going through a tough time. Perhaps you contributed to a colleague's fundraiser or helped a family member in need. Or you might have invested in an experience—a trip, a class, or a shared activity—that created lasting memories with those you care about. This builds relationship wealth, as we discussed in the previous chapter.

Kelly had always been careful with money, but she realized her caution was leading to isolation. She rarely went out with friends because dining at restaurants felt too expensive. She declined invitations to events that required tickets or travel. While she was definitely saving money, but she was also preventing herself from connecting with others.

"I was so focused on not wasting money that I forgot money could help me build the relationships I truly wanted," she told me.

So Kelly made a deliberate change. She opened a new savings account called her connection fund, specifically designated for experiences shared with others. Concert tickets. Weekend trips with her sister. Hosting dinner parties instead of always meeting at coffee shops.

The result wasn't just stronger friendships but also a transformed relationship with money. "I stopped viewing spending as a failure and began seeing it as an investment in the life I actually wanted to live," she said.

She also began thinking beyond her immediate circle. She started making a monthly donation to an organization working on climate change because it felt like turning her values into action. She joined a giving circle with other women in her community, pooling resources to support local nonprofits.

"I realized my money could be part of something bigger than just my own security," she said. "It could help create the kind of world I want to live in."

When you view money as a tool for change, every financial decision becomes an opportunity to align with your values. You might choose to bank with institutions that invest in communities you care about, buy from businesses owned by people whose success you want to support, or invest in companies developing solutions to problems that matter to you.

All your financial choices serve as votes for the type of economy, community, and future you want to help build.

Sometimes, it involves spending a bit more to support a local business instead of a large corporation. Other times, it means investing in funds that evaluate environmental or social impact. Sometimes, it involves setting aside money specifically for giving, whether through formal donations or by helping people in your life when they need it.

The power lies in the intention behind it. When you use money as a bridge between your values and your actions, you create alignment that extends beyond your bank account.

Money As a Mirror

When you start viewing money as a resource rather than just an emergency stash, you begin to use it differently. You choose a gym membership over takeout. You spend on experiences that restore you, not just on the essentials that keep you going. You invest in companies solving problems you care about, not just because you can afford it, but because it aligns with your values.

Before we move on, though, we need to address the phrase *experiences that restore you*. Doing restorative activities does not make you temporarily lazy. Restoration is essential for realigning yourself and becoming even more productive moving forward. Taking a pause may be exactly what you need to determine your next step.

In moments of pause, money stops being just a tool for survival and instead becomes a means to express your intentions. It's perfectly acceptable to seek stability, but it's equally valid to desire beauty, freedom, and joy. You don't need to justify every expense with logic or productivity. Sometimes, the most meaningful use of money is the one that brings you closer to your true self.

When money becomes a living, breathing part of your life, not something you avoid or obsess over, you start to create space. And within that space, you discover choice. And choice is where your power lives.

Still, too many women delay taking financial action because they believe they are behind. They wait to learn more, save more, or feel more confident. Many others before you didn't begin with a perfect plan. They began with one step—uncertain, imperfect, but important. You don't need to read every book or master every investment strategy before you start. You don't need to overhaul your entire financial life all at once. You just need to begin.

Maybe that looks like opening a new savings account.

Maybe it's asking HR about your retirement options.

Maybe it's having an honest conversation with your partner.

Whatever it is, it counts.

There's no such thing as behind. There's only here. And progress starts here. Financial confidence doesn't show up overnight. It builds strength through repetition, consistency, and challenge. You begin with what you can manage and then stretch yourself when you're ready. Many women expect to leap from financial anxiety to complete mastery in a single step. But confidence doesn't work that way. It grows by showing up, layer by layer.

Your journey might begin with the exercises in this book. As you progress, concepts like investing, saving, and financial growth may become more complex, but they'll also feel more manageable. And this process won't all happen at once. It's about steady, deliberate movement in the direction you want to go.

Every decision you make and every action you take, even the small ones, strengthen your financial muscles. Checking your bank statements. Asking questions when something feels confusing. Choosing not to spend on things that don't align with your values. These daily habits add up. The confidence you seek doesn't come from knowing everything. It comes from trusting that you'll figure things out. That you'll make mistakes and adjust. That you'll keep showing up.

Start where you are. Build on what works. Give yourself credit, even when the progress feels invisible. You're not waiting for the perfect moment. You're already in it.

Exercise: Legacy Timeline

Legacy starts now with what you choose to build, share, and stand for moving forward.

Every decision you make with your time, money, and energy shapes your future influence. You're setting examples. You're teaching values. You're creating impact whether you intend to or not.

This exercise gives you the opportunity to pause and intentionally identify what you want to leave behind. Not just for your family but also for your community, your work, and the future you care about.

You've done the work to understand your past. Now, this is where you decide what comes next.

Grab another blank sheet of paper or use the space provided, and draw a horizontal line starting at today, extending as far into the future as you can imagine—two years, ten years, thirty years, or even three generations—whatever timeframe makes the most sense for you to think about now.

This is your Legacy Timeline—a map of what you want to build, shape, teach, and leave behind.

Step 1: Mark Key Future Milestones

Plot the moments that matter most. Think big; think deeply. Here are a few prompts to help:

- When do you want to make major shifts in how you use, invest, or give money?
- What impact do you want to have on your family, your community, and your field of work?
- Are there any projects, businesses, causes, or traditions you want to start (or end)?
- What do you want to model for those watching you?
- What story do you want people to tell about you one hundred years from now?

Mark each milestone with a date or age and jot down a short note or symbol to indicate what it represents.

Step 2: Name Your Legacy Themes

Once your timeline is filled in, step back and ask:

- What are the core values running through your future?
- What do these plans say about your definition of wealth?
- Where do you need to take bold action? Where do you need to slow down and listen?
- What might need to change today to make this vision real?

This timeline is about intention.

It's your chance to write the next chapter on purpose, not by default.

And if your legacy feels too big for one lifetime? Good. That means it's worth building.

Chapter Ten

Put It All into Practice

Until now, we've explored the origins of your limiting beliefs about money, and data shows that these beliefs are not your fault. They are often inherited, passed down through generations, and shaped by family, culture, trauma, and survival. You have reflected on where these beliefs took root in your life. We also discussed money guilt, the tendency to shrink yourself to stay safe, and practical ways to be bolder.

We redefined wealth not as a number, but as a life aligned with your values. We completed exercises in the Reflection and Connection sections to understand your emotional responses to money and transform them into clarity and action. And we saw by examples how the intentional use of money becomes a tool to create the life you truly desire.

Now it's time to bring it all together and complete your own personal financial philosophy™ (PFP) worksheet.

Let's revisit the exercise from Chapter 1. Review what you wrote down before reading this book, then redo the exercise using what you have learned in this book to help create your plan moving forward.

PUT IT ALL INTO PRACTICE

Mapping the Future

Find a comfortable seat and take a few deep, cleansing breaths.

Then answer these questions without censoring, judgement, or criticism. Just write (or think through if you aren't in a good place to write) whatever comes to mind. I suggest listing three but you may have more or less.

List three of the biggest mindset shifts you have enjoyed since starting this book.

_____

_____

_____

List three things you believe still haven't been acted on and need to change. Is there something you don't know or understand that you want to clarify before moving forward?

_____

_____

_____

List three things that map out the future you would like to have now that you are empowered with this new financial mindset.

_____

_____

_____

Why Mapping the Future Matters Now

Having a personal financial philosophy is more than just a nice idea. It is a powerful tool. It provides clarity on what truly matters so that every decision you make around money is grounded in your values, not fears or assumptions. Without a guiding philosophy, it is easy to default to what others expect or to fall into old habits that no longer serve you. A PFP is your compass. It may not dictate exactly what to do in every situation, but it keeps you oriented toward what's meaningful.

Without this kind of clarity, it's far too easy to fall back into old patterns. To spend out of pressure. To save out of fear. To wait for permission. Without a guiding framework, you end up building a financial life that might look good on paper but doesn't feel aligned. You chase someone else's version of success instead of pursuing your own.

That's why this moment matters. If you feel tempted to set this aside and come back to it later, that's completely normal. But pause and notice that impulse. That hesitation—that instinct to delay or downplay your own clarity—is exactly why this step is so important.

Life won't suddenly slow down, and you won't magically wake up with more time or confidence. The idea that you'll get to it when things calm down is often just another way of avoiding the discomfort of starting. But this work isn't about being perfect. It's about being present. The very act of writing your PFP is a signal to yourself: I am participating. I am paying attention. I am choosing to be in a relationship with my money.

You don't need a finance degree. You don't need a spreadsheet full of formulas. What you need is a connection to what matters—and that's what you've been building all along.

Think of this as a foundation you can return to again and again. Your PFP is not set in stone. It's a living document that grows with you. It evolves as your life evolves, providing something most people never take the time to create: a personal filter for every financial decision you make. It helps you stay anchored when the noise gets loud and guides you to know what's right for you, even when the world says otherwise.

You are more ready than you think. You have done the work to understand your patterns, untangle your guilt, and step into agency. Now is the time to shape what's next—not by following someone else's rules but by writing your own.

Developing Your Personal Financial Philosophy

Creating your PFP is about more than setting goals or making a budget. It's about taking complete authorship of your financial life. For many of us, money has felt like something that happens to us or around us. This worksheet gives you a chance to change that dynamic. It helps you decide how you want money to support your life instead of being driven by external expectations or old fears.

Your PFP offers a clear lens for making choices. When life feels overwhelming or decisions seem unclear, you can return to this page to remind yourself of what really matters. It acts as your guiding lens. The values you identify, the priorities you set, and the habits you develop all serve as reminders that you're not just going through the motions. You're making decisions with purpose.

The beauty of a PFP lies in its flexibility. It evolves as you do, allowing for change and growth. Most importantly, it keeps your well-being at the heart of your financial life. You don't need to follow someone else's system or meet predefined benchmarks to be on the right track. This is your guide, your blueprint, your unique version of alignment.

Writing everything down on paper gives you a powerful sense of control. You're saying: I get to define success for myself. I get to choose how I spend, save, give, and grow. I get to use money as a tool that supports me rather than a constraint that limits me. This kind of clarity is a form of wealth in itself.

This also highlights the importance of living your legacy now, not postponing joy, rest, or fulfillment for the sake of sacrifice.

I've heard people say, "I'm not going to fly coach my whole life just so my kids can fly first class after I'm gone." This serves as a reminder that building a meaningful life doesn't always mean holding back for someone else's future. Yes, generational wealth matters, but so does demonstrating what it means to live well, give generously, and spend intentionally—in the present.

Now, let's create the PFP worksheet that ties everything together. It's not about having every answer or achieving perfection. Instead, it's about making a clear, honest guide that reflects what matters most to you right now. Your personal financial philosophy should be simple, flexible, and deeply personal. It's something you can revisit and refine as your values evolve and your life continues to grow.

The worksheet is one page, structured into five main boxes across the top and center, followed by three smaller boxes at the bottom. Each section prompts you to think intentionally and holistically about your relationship with money. You can fill in the one provided here or if you want a bigger version, please go to my website at www.marciadawood.com/wealth to download a free copy.

PERSONAL FINANCIAL PHILOSOPHY WORKSHEET

My Aligned Values

What Will Money Make Possible For Me?

My Top Three Financial Priorities

Habits I Will Release

Habits I Want to Adopt Moving Forward

Planning the Future

6 Month Plan

1 Year Plan

5 Year Plan

Put It All into Practice

The Five Main Boxes:

1. **My Aligned Values**

Write down the values that guide your life and describe how you want your money to support those values. These could be things like freedom, security, generosity, creativity, or connection.

2. **What Will Money Make Possible for Me?**

Think about the real-life impact of financial clarity. What do you want to do if you could handle money more easily? Travel more? Be present for your family? Start a business?

3. **My Top Three Financial Priorities**

List your current top financial goals. These might include paying off debt, building an emergency fund, investing for retirement, or saving for something meaningful.

4. **Habits I Will Release**

Consider the habits or thought patterns that have held you back. This might be avoiding financial conversations, people-pleasing with money, or constantly second-guessing your spending.

5. **Habits I Want to Adopt Moving Forward**

Identify supportive habits you want to cultivate. This could include checking in weekly with your money, asking questions when you don't understand something, or celebrating financial wins.

The Three Planning the Future Boxes:

At the bottom of the worksheet, set some goals. What do you think is possible to do in the next six months? In the next year? And in the next five years?

This worksheet isn't about perfection. It's a snapshot of who you are, what you value, and how you want to navigate your financial life with greater confidence, calm, and clarity. Keep it visible. Let it evolve. And trust that you are fully capable of living by it.

CLOSING THOUGHTS: LIVE YOUR LEGACY NOW

There are moments in life when a decision becomes a turning point. You begin to see yourself differently. You stop waiting to feel ready. You move forward because you know the cost of staying silent is too high.

Katharine Graham faced a moment like this. The stakes were historic, with a decision before her that would shape not only a story but also the legacy of her business. She needed to decide whether to back a controversial story. She stood at a crossroads, weighing the impact on her company, her reputation, and everything that her family had built.

She chose to publish.

That story became Watergate.

And it brought down a president.

But before she made that decision, Katharine Graham had to endure her own fire.

She was never supposed to lead. Her father, Eugene Meyer, bought *The Washington Post* in 1933, but when he stepped down, he handed the paper to her husband, Philip. Not to her. Because women didn't run companies. They didn't inherit businesses. They didn't sit at the table. They hosted dinner parties, wore pretty dresses, and raised children.

In 1963, Philip died by suicide after a long battle with mental illness and alcoholism. Suddenly, at forty-six, Katharine became the publisher of a struggling newspaper. She lacked business training. She was surrounded by men who doubted her. And she doubted herself.

In her early years as a publisher, she experienced deep and persistent self-doubt. In her memoir, she attributed this insecurity to "the narrow way women's roles were defined," writing that "we had been brought up ... to think that we were put on the earth to make men happy and comfortable." As a woman in a male-dominated field, she had "no female role models and faced difficulty being taken seriously by many of her male colleagues and employees."

In the documentary, *Becoming Katharine Graham*, she said: "The worst handicap women work under is the self-inflicted one—that if you have grown up thinking of yourself as a second-class citizen, you tend to always put yourself down."

That quote stopped me in my tracks because, in many ways, we remain in the same place today.

We live in a moment of historic opportunity. We can own wealth. We can run companies. We can rewrite the rules. But too many of us are still dragging around inherited beliefs—scarcity stories passed down from generations of women who had to play small just to survive.

So, we hesitate. We doubt. We apologize for taking up space and wanting more.

This is the cultural crossroads we have discussed throughout this book: the meeting of limiting beliefs from the past and the unlimited potential of now. On one side, the women who came before us—brilliant, fierce, and resourceful—but held back by a world that didn't fully recognize or appreciate them. On the other side lies a world where we can lead boldly, on our own terms.

Mindset matters. We must change our internal narrative. If we don't, we risk recreating the same limitations, even as external barriers are gradually removed.

Katharine Graham did more than shift the narrative—she rewrote it.

Closing Thoughts: Live Your Legacy Now

In June 1972, five men were arrested for breaking into the Democratic National Committee headquarters at the Watergate complex in Washington, D.C. At first, it seemed like a strange, isolated burglary. But *The Washington Post* reporters Bob Woodward and Carl Bernstein kept digging.

What they uncovered was far more significant: a sprawling web of political espionage, illegal wiretaps, hush money, and cover-ups, extending all the way to the Nixon White House.

As the story developed, so did the pressure. The Nixon administration launched attacks on *The Post*, threatened legal action, and attempted to discredit the reporters. Advertisers were anxious. Board members were concerned. Other media outlets hesitated to get involved.

Katharine Graham was still a relatively new publisher and privately doubted herself, but she made the decision to stand behind her newsroom. She published the stories. She ignored the threats. She chose the truth.

That decision led to congressional hearings, public outrage, and ultimately the resignation of President Richard Nixon in August 1974. It wasn't just a victory for journalism—it was a watershed moment for democracy. And this outcome occurred because one woman refused to fold.

Ironically, three-time Oscar-winning actor Meryl Streep, who has openly shared her own struggles with self-doubt, portrayed Katharine Graham in the film *The Post*. Reflecting on Graham's evolution from uncertainty to influence, Streep noted how deeply her upbringing and the expectations of her era shaped her. "She was not the confident Katharine Graham that people came to know as the first female head of a Fortune 500 company. She was someone very unsure of herself." Streep went on to say, "Katharine Graham was someone who was a product of her time. It was the whole culture that undermined all women, especially women that should've had the most agency of all—highly educated, wealthy women who had every opportunity to step into important places in life, but they sat back."

Despite all the challenges, cultural norms, and moments of self-doubt, Graham prevailed. Under her leadership, The Washington Post Company's stock increased by more than 3,000 percent. She expanded the business by adding television stations and acquiring *Newsweek* magazine. She also built a strong relationship with Warren Buffett, who became a major shareholder and trusted advisor, someone she relied on for financial guidance in a rapidly changing media landscape.

She rose above mere survival and scaled her business to success. She proved that it is entirely possible to lead with principle and strength, combining integrity with extraordinary effectiveness.

Additionally, she passed down her beliefs to the next generation.

In 2012, I had the privilege of meeting her son, Don Graham. At that time, I was working for Kaplan Education, which was owned by *The Washington Post*. Don visited our Charlotte, North Carolina, campus to learn more about the various holdings within what was now his company. The college was managed by a woman, and I was her regional manager.

What struck me wasn't just who he was, but how he showed up. He didn't march in like an executive with an agenda. Instead, he sat with the staff. He listened to students. He asked questions. He paid close attention. There was no ego—only curiosity, humility, and a deep respect for the mission of education.

That experience stayed with me.

It made me realize that Katharine Graham didn't just transform an institution; she also passed down her values. Leadership wasn't something she modeled once and then left behind. It became a legacy. Courage, humility, and a refusal to play small—they lived on in her son. And they can live on in us as well.

That same courage and clarity are not just for boardrooms or breaking newsrooms. They also guide how we lead our lives, shape our futures, and relate to a reality as fundamental and powerful as money.

Closing Thoughts: Live Your Legacy Now

And yes, women are good with money, even though we often don't believe we are.

We've been conditioned not to trust ourselves with money. We've inherited guilt, outdated stories, and unspoken cultural messages that encourage us to step back rather than take charge. Girls are often told they're not good at math, and over time, math becomes linked with money. Consequently, money becomes something we tend to avoid.

We internalize these beliefs until they feel like facts. Then, we wonder why it feels uncomfortable to earn more, invest, lead, or pursue financial independence unapologetically.

This is about more than money. It's about power, agency, and possibility.

Throughout this book, we've explored the beliefs many of us as women have carried: beliefs passed down through generations, shaped by silence, and never our fault. And we've also discussed what becomes possible when you begin to rewrite those stories. When you choose to align your money with your values and lead with boldness. This is your moment. No one needs to grant you permission. The role is already yours to claim. Trust your voice. It's time to move forward.

Financial fluidity isn't about chasing a perfect goal or hitting arbitrary milestones. It's about using money as a tool to build a life that aligns with your values. It's about being able to make intentional choices rather than reactive ones. To step forward, to scale back, to pause or pivot when life demands it—without everything falling apart.

It's not about getting every decision right. It's about building a foundation strong enough to support what matters most through seasons of growth, uncertainty, reinvention, and rest.

We're not here in this life to inherit shame. We're not here to stay stuck in scarcity. We're not here to carry guilt for wanting more.

We are here to be the main character of our own Hollywood movie.

When you step into that role, stop waiting, stop apologizing, and finally claim the space you were meant for, and you will begin to see the world differently.

You wake up in the morning with a sense of ease. You move with intention. Your decisions feel clearer, no longer clouded by fear or constant second-guessing. You speak up without anticipating pushback, knowing you're not the only one finding your voice. More women are living this way now, and that momentum is driving change. The world around you is beginning to shift, becoming more aligned, more responsive, and better equipped to meet you where you are.

You ask for what you want, not because you must prove yourself but because you know you deserve it.

You stop shrinking yourself to make others comfortable. Instead, you expand to reach your full potential. You trust your instincts. You say yes to what excites you, and you say no without guilt or explanation. And you don't care if the laundry is folded or if there are still chores to be done—sometimes, those things can just wait.

You no longer cling to what's familiar just because it feels safe. You let go of what no longer serves you, not because it's easy, but because you finally trust yourself to stand on your own foundation.

Self-doubt never fully disappears—not for Katharine Graham, not for Meryl Streep, and not for you. The inner critic doesn't simply pack up and leave once you step into your power. Self-doubt will still arise, sometimes during moments that matter most, sometimes on an ordinary Wednesday afternoon. But when you've built a foundation of trust in yourself, doubt becomes background noise instead of the narrator of your story.

This is no longer survival. This is design. This is power.

We are here to build. To lead. To create wealth, voice, and impact—unapologetically. This is the only way we will rewrite the centuries-old stories we have inherited, replacing them with new narratives of possibility, choice, and power.

Closing Thoughts: Live Your Legacy Now

You don't have to wait until you feel ready. You don't have to silence yourself to be accepted. The world doesn't need another woman playing small. It needs you to take the seat. Make the call. Move forward like it matters—because it does. When you do, you build a life you love that's fully your own, leaving behind a blueprint for the generations who will rise after you.

AUTHOR'S NOTE

Money is an emotional subject. It shapes our choices, opportunities, and even how we see ourselves. Throughout this book, I share stories, insights, and lessons about money—how we think about it, how we use it, and, most importantly, how we can shift our mindset to build the financial future we truly desire.

To protect individuals' privacy, I have changed names and certain details in the stories I share. While the lessons are real, some specifics have been modified to maintain confidentiality.

This book is intended for informational purposes only and should not be taken as legal, tax, accounting, or investment advice. At the time of writing, I serve on the U.S. Securities and Exchange Commission (SEC) Small Business Capital Formation Advisory Committee; however, the views expressed here are my own and do not represent those of the SEC or my fellow committee members. Before making any significant financial decisions, I strongly encourage you to consult a qualified professional.

I have included data and research throughout the book, often citing sources directly within the text. You will find additional references in the endnotes if something sparks your curiosity.

Above all, this book is about taking action to transform our thoughts and beliefs about money. I share both my own experiences and those of others—so you can learn, adapt, and take control of your financial future. Imagine the impact if more people made even small, intentional shifts in their money mindset. It wouldn't just change individual lives—it could transform entire communities.

RESOURCES

The accompanying workbook for *Unapologetic Wealth* offers expanded exercises, action plans, and extra tools to help you develop these skills systematically and monitor your progress over time. It is available wherever you purchase books.

Marcia is the host of *The Angel Next Door* podcast, which helps to demystify all things related to angel investing and reimagine what wealth really is: a tool to rewrite your money story to create a life you love. Listen wherever you get your podcasts, and you can watch and listen on YouTube.

And visit www.marciadawood.com for many free resources as well.

A Favor

I could use your help! If you have gotten value from this book, would you take a minute or two to share your thoughts in a review? Reviews are so meaningful to the success of a book, its reach, and its impact. I would greatly appreciate your support.

> Let's start a conversation.
> Reach out to me on social media.
> www.marciadawood.com
> @marciadawood on IG
> marciadawood on LinkedIn

ACKNOWLEDGMENTS

I never set out to write one book—let alone two. But books have a unique way of changing people. They meet us in private, challenge our perceptions of what is possible, and often say the things we didn't know we needed to hear. Our relationship with books is personal, powerful, and sometimes even transformational.

I wrote this one because it needed to exist. So many people, especially women, have told me they want to invest, to align their money with their values, and take control of their financial lives… but they don't know where to start. *Unapologetic Wealth* is the prequel to *Do Good While Doing Well* because, before we can do good with our money, we must believe we're allowed to build wealth in the first place.

My hope is that this book, and the accompanying workbook, give people that starting point—and the confidence to keep going.

I wouldn't have had the knowledge, the experiences, or the opportunities to write this if it weren't for my husband, Izzy. His outlook on money and on life is refreshing, generous, and full of joy. He makes everything more fun. Thank you, Izzy, for always being my biggest supporter and cheerleader.

To my parents: thank you for making money a normal and open topic from the very beginning. My mom found a way to be present at home while still working hard, and my dad never let money become a taboo subject.

Losing my mom to ALS left a permanent mark on my heart. Watching her fight a disease with no cure is something I'll never forget, and it's part of what drives me. I stay passionate about helping others find purpose and possibility in their financial journeys, because life is too short not to. And I'll continue to support efforts to find treatments and, one day, a cure for ALS and other devastating diseases. That's part of what building wealth is about: using it to make a difference where it matters most.

A huge thank you once again to AJ Harper and Laura Stone for your wisdom, encouragement, and for creating the incredible Top Three Book (T3) community, which is full of so many amazing people like Vickie Lanthier and Kristina Paider. I absolutely could not have written *this* book without AJ. If you're thinking about writing a book, do yourself a favor: read her book, *Write a Must-Read*, and dive into everything she offers online. It will transform your process and your perspective.

I'm deeply grateful to everyone who allowed me to share their money stories in this book. Thank you for trusting me with your experiences and for giving others the chance to see themselves in your journey.

And thank you to my beta readers. Your insights helped shape this book: Carolyn Jungclas, Melissa Goff, Amanda Gibson, Natalie Siston, Irena Asmundson, Brittany Barreto, Arnee Gomez, Lara Zibners, Colleen Surmay, Amber Fain, Jules Apollo, Rich Palmer, Eva Doss, Beth Smith, Marjorie Mahalingam, Nancy Hayes, Lindsay Cappello, Gail Nastasia, Kelly Ann Winget, Syama Bunten, Monika Gnuess, Sandra Hughes, Kristina Montague, Lucy Turnage, Danielle Schulz, Sally Boulter, Julie Ellis, and Amy Jacobs.

A special and heartfelt thank you to Sue Bevan Baggott for your generous wisdom, thoughtful feedback, and steady support on this shared journey to bring the innovations we believe in to life.

AUTHOR BIO

Marcia Dawood is an angel investor, advocate for financial empowerment, and a leading voice in early-stage investing. She serves as chair of the SEC's Small Business Capital Formation Advisory Committee and is a venture partner with Mindshift Capital. Marcia is also chair emeritus of the Angel Capital Association (ACA), a global professional society of angel investors, and a longtime member of Golden Seeds. As the founding chair of the ACA's Growing Women's Capital Group, she is helping to build a stronger ecosystem of support for women-led companies across the U.S.

She is the author of the multi-award-winning book *Do Good While Doing Well: Invest for Change, Reap Financial Rewards, and Increase Your Happiness*, along with its accompanying workbook.

Marcia is also an associate producer of the multi-award-winning documentary *Show Her the Money*, a TEDx speaker, and the host of the award-winning *The Angel Next Door* podcast. She has invested in more than fifty early-stage companies and funds, with a focus on diverse founders tackling some of the world's biggest challenges.

Earlier in her career, Marcia spent more than sixteen years in leadership roles at Kaplan Education, focusing on sales, marketing, and operations. She holds an MBA from the University of North Carolina's Kenan-Flagler Business School.

She lives in North Carolina with her husband, Izzy, and feels grateful to be the stepmother of three wonderful sons.

REFERENCES

i https://www.bankrate.com/loans/personal-loans/history-of-women-and-loans/

ii https://www.mckinsey.com/industries/financial-services/our-insights/women-as-the-next-wave-of-growth-in-us-wealth-management

iii https://newsroom.wf.com/English/news-releases/news-release-details/2024/New-Report-Finds-Growth-of-Women-Business-Owners-Outpaces-the-Market/#:~:text=According%20to%20the%202024%20Wells,growth%20increased%20to%204.5%20times.&text=Whether%20it%20was%20during%20COVID,the%20$1%20million%20revenue%20threshold.

iv https://www.mckinsey.com/industries/financial-services/our-insights/women-as-the-next-wave-of-growth-in-us-wealth-management

v https://www.stlouisfed.org/on-the-economy/2025/mar/pension-401k-retirement-plan-trends-us-workplace

vi https://www.cbsnews.com/news/payless-sold-discount-shoes-at-luxury-prices-and-it-worked/

vii https://www.youtube.com/watch?v=_7VEWTbe5lU&t=3s

viii https://www.mckinsey.com/featured-insights/diversity-and-inclusion/women-in-the-workplace&https://www.cultureamp.com/blog/microaggressions-at-work

ix https://www.fidelity.ca/en/insights/articles/womenandinvesting/

x   https://dn790002.ca.archive.org/0/items/DanielKahneman
    ThinkingFastAndSlow/Daniel%20Kahneman-Thinking
    %2C%20Fast%20and%20Slow%20%20.pdf
xi https://www.alexbrown.com/kenneysyracusebell/resources/
    behavioral-finance/loss-aversion

www.ingramcontent.com/pod-product-compliance
Lightning Source LLC
LaVergne TN
LVHW020434070526
838199LV00032B/628/J